GREAT DISCOVERIES IN SCIENCE

Gravity

by Kevin Czarnecki

Cavendish Square

New York

Published in 2017 by Cavendish Square Publishing, LLC
243 5th Avenue, Suite 136, New York, NY 10016

First Edition

Website: cavendishsq.com

This publication represents the opinions and views of the author based on his or her personal experience, knowledge, and research. The information in this book serves as a general guide only. The author and publisher have used their best efforts in preparing this book and disclaim liability rising directly or indirectly from the use and application of this book.

CPSIA Compliance Information: Batch #CS16CSQ

All websites were available and accurate when this book was sent to press.

Library of Congress Cataloging-in-Publication Data

Names: Czarnecki, Kevin R., 1983- author.
Title: Gravity / Kevin R. Czarnecki.
Description: New York: Cavendish Square Publishing, [2017] |
Series: Great discoveries in science | Includes bibliographical references and index.
Identifiers: LCCN 2016009000 (print) | LCCN 2016012126 (ebook) |
ISBN 9781502619570 (library bound) | ISBN 9781502619587 (ebook)
Subjects: LCSH: Gravity--Juvenile literature.
Classification: LCC QC178 .C93 2017 (print) |
LCC QC178 (ebook) | DDC 531/.14--dc23
LC record available at http://lccn.loc.gov/2016009000

Editorial Director: David McNamara
Editor: Leah Tallon
Copy Editor: Michele Suchomel-Casey
Art Director: Jeffrey Talbot
Designer: Lindsey Auten
Production Assistant: Karol Szymczuk
Photo Research: J8 Media

The photographs in this book are used by permission and through the courtesy of: Mark Garlick/Getty Images, cover; 2xSamara.com/Shutterstock. com, 4; http://wellcomeimages.org/indexplus/obf_images/c8/2c/543811a5a95f1d23773146328125.jpg/File: Page from Edwin Smith surgical papyrus/ Wellcome L0051967.jpg/Wikimedia Commons, 8; DeAgostini/Getty Images, 12; Jastrow (2006)/Ludovisi Collection, National Museum of Rome, Palazzo Altemps/File: Aristotle Altemps Inv8575.jpg/Wikimedia Commons, 18; Universal History Archive/Getty Images, 21, 23, 52; Ullstein Bild/ Ullstein Bild via Getty Images, 25; Science Source, 28; http://wellcomeimages.org/indexplus/obf_images/3d/a4/fd53ee5769d7e8825d00adb31410.jpg/ File: Arithmetica musica Wellcome L0013221EB.jpg/Wikimedia Commons, 33; The Print Collector/Getty Images, 36, 64; NASA/http://www. hq.nasa.gov/alsj/a15/AS15-88-11890HR.jpg/File: Apollo 15 F&H.jpg/Wikimedia Commons, 37; Own work/Centraal Museum, Utrecht/File: Utrecht Weenix Descartes.JPG/Wikimedia Commons, 41; Cambridge University DSpace (http://www.dspace.cam.ac.uk/handle/1810/218646)/ File: Newton - 1677.jpeg/Wikimedia Commons, 44; From geograph.org.uk (http://www.geograph.org.uk/photo/1057094) Peter Church (http://www.geograph.org.uk/profile/16649)/File: Nevile's Court, Trinity College, Cambridge - geograph.org.uk - 1057094.jpg /Wikimedia Commons, 47; Ann Ronan Pictures/Print Collector/Getty Images, 49; Ferdinand Schmutzer (1870-1928)/ http://www.bhm.ch/de/news_04a. cfm?bid=4&jahr=2006/File: Einstein1921 by F Schmutzer 2.jpg /Wikimedia Commons, 54; AFP/Getty Images, 57; Underwood and Underwood, New York/Library of Congress/"Professor Einstein's Visit to the United States", The Scientific Monthly 12:5 (1921), 482-485, on p. 483. [1] (https://archive.org/stream/scientificmonthl12ameruoft#page/482/mode/2up)/File: Albert Einstein photo 1921.jpg /Wikimedia Commons, 62; Ted Kinsman / Science Source, 66; Peter Sobchak/File: Lunar Orbit and Orientation with respect to the Ecliptic.tif/Wikimedia Commons, 68; User: Dna-Dennis/File: NewtonsLawOfUniversalGravitation.svg/Wikimedia Commons, 69; NASA/http://spaceflight.nasa.gov/gallery/ images/shuttle/sts-122/html/s122e008922.html/File: S122e008922.jpg/Wikimedia Commons, 73; Andrey Armyagov /Shutterstock.com, 75; MARK GARLICK/SCIENCE PHOTO LIBRARY/Science Photo Library/Newscom, 82; Ralph Morse/The LIFE Picture Collection/Getty Images, 89; Hermann Luyken/File: 2014.11.15.141107 Maglev train Longyang Road Station Shanghai.jpg /Wikimedia Commons, 92; No machine-readable author provided. Zeimusu assumed (based on copyright claims)/File: Gravity assist moving Jupiter.svg - Wikimedia Commons, 93.

Printed in the United States of America

Contents

Many popular games have rules based on gravity.

Introduction: What Goes Up ...

Gravity. The single most present, influential, and powerful force in the universe. It defines all aspects of physical reality, yet from the everyday perspective, it is almost always thought of in its most immediate, observable form. This can be summed up in one famous phrase: What goes up, must come down.

It can be easy to get stuck in your own perspective and only see how gravity affects you in everyday life. You drop your books, and they hit the ground. You stumble on a crack in the sidewalk and fall down. But consider the influence gravity has in the grander sense. It's why a backpack is so heavy. It's why a car skids when it hits a patch of ice. Gravity affects all matter in all of known existence, and all of existence is formed based on the principle of the force it exerts. The design of the human body is a response to the environment, which is entirely shaped by gravity. Every breath taken, every beat of a heart, the sun in the sky, and the seasons passing by are all products of this force. The universe as we understand it could not exist without it.

Over two millennia would pass after an initial theory to explain gravity was proposed, and it went mostly unquestioned and unexamined. The beginning of all knowledge starts with questions, and it was a long time before anyone questioned the explanations they had been given. The fact is, gravity is easy to take for granted. We experience it constantly in all but the rarest of circumstances, much like breathing or sleeping. Sometimes it takes someone extraordinary to step back and question what we see every day. Often it takes a few people at the same time, asking the same question, to even begin to see the whole picture.

More than that, striking out from a position of ignorance is the hardest way of all. Originally, there was no previous research to base new conclusions on. Beginning a new course of study is always a slow process. But over time, with research, practice, and observation, results begin to show. The snowball effect of positive research takes hold, and before long a new school of understanding is born. It's the same for anyone who takes a leap and tries something different in science.

Today scientists have a profound understanding of gravitational sciences, which have come to affect technological and economic development all over the planet. From the weight ratios of shipping and fuel to new architectural feats of engineering to the design of rockets for spaceships and interstellar probes to our growing understanding of the cosmos, the study of gravity remains at the forefront of scientific progress. Perhaps the most wondrous (and intimidating) aspect of it all is how much is still unknown. The further we go, the further we can see ahead, and we begin to realize how much more there is to discover. New frontiers reveal themselves constantly, promising new and exciting advances in the coming years, some of which may change life in ways we never imagined.

Under ordinary circumstances, an examination of the science behind gravity and the associated physics at work in its theories would require a great deal of complex math to explain its mechanisms, which is, unfortunately, beyond the scope of this book. Instead, this text is meant as an introductory primer, in simple language, about just what gravity is, what it does, how it works, and where it is going in modern scientific development, as well as the history behind its discovery, the scientific schools of thought that led to it, and the people who played a part in understanding it first.

For some readers, this might be the first step on a new path to progressing the science of gravity. For others, this can offer a primer for understanding gravity, finally explaining why what goes up must come down.

The Edwin Smith Papyrus is one of the earliest scientific texts ever discovered.

UNPLACED FRAGMENTS

THE SURGICAL TREATISE, COLUMN I

CHAPTER 1

The Problem of Gravity

G ravity is very difficult to deny, considering the readily available evidence of its existence. An invisible force is present that exerts its influence to pull matter toward the ground. But imagine the world without an available answer as to why. What if you lived two thousand years ago and were asked to explain why things fall, and no one had ever heard the word "gravity" before? What would you believe? How would you reach your conclusion?

The FIRST STEPS

The first sparks of scientific thought may have originated in Egypt around 1600 BCE. There is evidence of advanced reasoning in recovered records, such as the Edwin Smith Papyrus, an ancient Egyptian medical text that is the oldest known surgical work in human history. The papyrus shows evidence of scientific thought that does not conflict with the inherent mysticism of the society of the time and endorses an empirical methodology. That is to say, it assumes nothing, looking for facts that are provable through observation and experience. This degree of sophistication is astounding, and unfortunately there are only a few bits of evidence left from ancient Egyptian civilization that we can use to learn more about their scientific practices, such as the Ebers Papyrus, from about 1550 BCE.

Many of the first millennium BCE's technological and scientific advances were at the hands of the Babylonians and the Egyptians, who used a combination of scientific and magical methods to achieve their goals, such as divination, which is the attempt to predict future events or see distant locations remotely. While the metaphysical or mystical aspect cannot be given any validity, it is important to note that it was a crucial motivating factor in their continual technical advancement. Complex mathematical formulas would be discovered in their quest to build grander temples or devise more "effective" magical circles. What they lacked, however, was an understanding of the underlying theories and facts about natural phenomena. They tried to use their mathematics to understand and describe nature, but without an abstract view to consider new angles of perception, it became impossible to define grander aspects of the universe and how they all tie together. This didn't stop them from making fantastic strides in discovery, though. In the words of historian Asger Aaboe, "all subsequent varieties of scientific astronomy, in the Hellenistic world, in India, in Islam, and in the West—if not indeed all subsequent endeavor in the exact sciences—depend upon Babylonian astronomy in decisive and fundamental ways." In other words, no matter what wrong turns were made later on, the essential core of all scientific thought to follow found its beginnings here.

GREEK INFLUENCES

The next great leap took place almost a thousand years after the Egyptians and across the Mediterranean Sea, when the Greek philosopher and mathematician Thales of Miletus took the first steps in recorded European history to separate the study of natural phenomena from mythology. At the time, it was a revolutionary concept. No one had ever sought answers to questions about the way the world worked through anything other than magical, often religious explanation. These earliest scientific methods were developed in sixth-century Greece. The term "science" can only be used loosely, however. These first researchers sought answers to the mysteries of the physical world but utilized philosophical methods rather than scientific ones. This means that they developed theories and then sought evidence to support their hypotheses, rather than utilizing tests and observation to find repeatable processes and explanations for why they worked. For this reason, they were known as natural philosophers, rather than scientists. These philosophers did take steps toward true empirical thought, however. Anaximander, a Greek philosopher, further clarified the idea by imposing the idea of law onto observed research. He felt that there must be a sense of consistent rules that governed research and discovery, and that once something was established, it should be added to these laws.

A light of hope came from one of the earliest great Greek philosophers, however. Parmenides established two standards that keep sophistry from becoming a pure debating art:

- The goal of philosophy should not be the theoretical but pursuing actual fact and utilizing the technique of logic.
- It is certain that any conclusion is the result of a theory so that a connection between the two can be made and supported.

Education for anyone in those days was not formalized, lacking even the structure of an apprenticeship system. In the century to follow, a new kind of philosopher, the sophist, would

A bust of Parmenides, an early
Greek philosopher.

emerge, traveling from town to town and offering tutelage to the sons of rich men in exchange for money. This education was largely an oral tradition, consisting of long conversations where questions were asked and answers were challenged. While this was quite helpful in preparing young men for debate and fostering persuasiveness through logical debate, it also had the effect of a game of "telephone," where different teachers might develop different theories and explanations for the arguments they had with their students, and vice versa. Ideas and theories would mutate as they spread, changing like a rumor from person to person, so that there was no hope of a unified scientific view on topics. Without that unity of thought, it became that much more difficult to progress theories in any meaningful way.

What's more, the practical application of discoveries remained limited. For example, fifth-century BCE Greeks had their first encounter with magnetism in the form of iron oxide, which they referred to as lodestone. They observed its ability to pull small pieces of iron to itself. Around the same time, it was found that when amber was rubbed with fur it could attract bits of straw and small feathers to itself. Today we recognize this as an occurrence of static electricity, but at the time, it was merely a curiosity. Indeed, magnets would be nothing but a source of mild amusement for more than a thousand years, until their use in the development of the compass.

The NATURAL PHILOSOPHER

In many ways, it may seem strange that the natural philosophers did not take a greater interest in these astounding events or seek greater knowledge of the processes that made them happen. To understand why, it is important to bear in mind the world the philosophers inhabited. Ancient, often superstitious beliefs were accepted as reality. Lightning was

The Life of a Sophist

For a wandering teacher, life was a matter of seeking patronage. The sophist would seek an early education, gathering knowledge from reputable (or at least famous) teachers, basically padding his résumé while learning the art of debate, as well as any information that might enhance his ability to make an argument. From there, he struck out for the cities and settlements that might have young, wealthy men, often the scions of aristocratic families, who would pay for an education.

Once a patron was found, the sophist could grow quite wealthy in his own right. Lessons were as much a matter of presenting facts and parables as engaging in active questioning, both to foster a deeper understanding of the subject as well as learning to look at it from new angles. Hours each day were spent in contemplation of fables and tales, historical events and personal anecdotes, as well as logic puzzles and riddles, debating the perspectives of history, the morals of parables, or the merits of philosophies.

While the idea of knowledge and wisdom were appealing in their own right, the sophist offered something far more interesting: *arete*, which means virtue or excellence. Once, it had meant intelligence and the benevolent use of it for others, but around the fifth century BCE, it had changed in meaning, becoming the descriptor for those who could (and would) manipulate others with their learning. The very word "sophistry" has come to mean "the use of reasoning or arguments that sound correct but are actually false." Many had come to see the sophist as doing little more than teach would-be politicians how to lie more effectively and almost always for their own gain.

not a byproduct of physical events, but the will of the gods. The priests and priestesses of ancient Greece's many cultures maintained a popular and unopposed grip on the theological imagination of its citizens, with many philosophers subtly influenced to agree. Perhaps worse, Parmenides's logical method was used in the reverse of modern scientific theory: devise a solution for something, and then work backward to discover evidence that supports that hypothesis.

To better grasp how that kind of logic works, let's apply it to another kind of mystery. Imagine you are a police officer. You are called to investigate a robbery, where a safe has been cracked and jewels have been taken. As an officer of the law, your job is to investigate the crime scene for clues and perhaps figure out how the crime was committed. If you do your work like a natural philosopher, you might come up with an idea as to how the thief got into the house, broke into the safe, and escaped, then search for evidence that supports your theory. As a result, you aren't as open to other ways the crime might have happened and may miss additional clues that go against your hypothesis. A cop today would use a more impartial scientific method to find all the clues possible, then use those to construct a theory from there. This underlines the essential difference between the philosophical and scientific methods: the philosopher assumes a solution and seeks evidence, while the scientist analyzes evidence and seeks a solution, assuming nothing.

Just the same, these natural philosophers were the early pioneers of science, studying nature and developing the basic building blocks of how to understand the world outside of theological explanation. As it was an early model, the philosophers worked with what they knew, dividing all matter into its four elements: earth, air, fire, and water. Each element had its place in the universe, and every kind of material could fit into those classifications based on their position in nature.

Earth was at the bottom, with water above it, as water flows over riverbeds. Above that was air, and above that fire, based on the position of the sun above all else. Different objects would have different compositions of those elements and would therefore seek to find their natural place in the universe. Hence, a stone would fall to the ground with its own kind, while fire seemed to rise up to the sky, reaching for the sun. A less pure material would move to a point in between or rise or fall more slowly. A feather, for example, would have a high proportion of air. Since birds are creatures that fly, and feathers come from birds, it stood to reason that feathers had the same admixture of air and would float to the ground slowly or be swept up by a gentle breeze. By this logic, an object's composition could partially be determined by its weight, so it was believed that a heavier object should and would fall faster than a lighter object.

Many of these ideas would come about around 320 BCE, as research was cataloged and categorized, dividing the natural philosophies into different schools of thought, such as physics, biology, and even poetry. With this came the assertion that you must be able to prove your theory through demonstration rather than faith. Once something was known, it could be applied to other theories, allowing for the building of knowledge from one idea to the next. This meant that natural philosophy, rather than being a series of disconnected ideas and experiments, could now form a basis of knowledge that would inform new ideas and theories, developing into proper schools of thought in which one might specialize and excel. It also meant that documented ideas and discoveries could be passed from one philosopher to another without relying on word of mouth. So long as the writing was accurate, many students could profit by having access to the same knowledge. This meant more and more knowledge was gathered and categorized, scrolls passing between teachers and to students, and large collections could be stored. In 200 BCE, this would reach a new pinnacle as the first cataloged library in Western civilization would be established at Alexandria.

While this might seem like a very obvious and slow progression of ideas, these were revolutionary ideas in their times. Much like a snowball rolling downhill, science began to accumulate and gain in size, growing larger and gaining more momentum all the time. Before long, scholars and philosophers would make pilgrimages not only to learn from masters of their disciplines, but they would also travel to these great repositories of knowledge to study and share new ideas inspired by them.

It would be hundreds of years before this system of learning and examination was questioned, let alone evolved into new forms of inquiry. Around the fifth century BCE full-fledged schools had begun teaching math and geometry. Historically famous figures such as Plato and his student Aristotle took the stage and introduced their own components to the emerging scientific tradition. Aristotle, in particular, developed a method of induction and deduction. In essence, it was the analysis and classification of all facts related to a subject, then deducing their connections and effects on each other. Induction meant studying many observations of a subject to form a reasonable idea of its possibilities, while deduction was figuring out what follows from that without needing to be demonstrated. One of the classic observations he made was, "All men are mortal. Socrates was a man. Therefore, Socrates was mortal." Aristotle's school of thought taught that the sophist accidentally discovered knowledge, but it was the natural philosopher's duty to discover universal truths and then explain how they worked. This method of established observation to shape conclusions and provoke further theories was far from foolproof but was nonetheless one of the most important tools for advancing scientific thought.

A bust of Aristotle, a naturalist philosopher.

Perhaps one of the more overlooked philosophies of the time, which had far-reaching influences, was Parmenides's denial of reality. He theorized that all elements of the world are interconnected and denied the separation of one element from another, claiming there was a component of reality that could not be observed and that might still influence the way in which we experience it. While this flew in the face of the separation of schools of science, it did open the imagination to forces that could not yet be measured and should still be taken into account. If nothing else, it would be necessary to consider that we do not yet have the entire picture, and the ongoing arguments it would inspire ensured the continual growth of curiosity and inquiry. This ensured that natural philosophers did not rest easy after reaching a conclusion and that science would continue to progress no matter how sure a solution appeared.

The next great steps would be taken in Islamic culture, almost a thousand years later in the eighth and ninth centuries CE, as Muslim scientists developed an increased focus on combining demonstration with theory. Their philosophy emphasized observation and precision, and many pursued the arts as a means to hone these twin qualities in their studies. One of their great advances was to compare different theories, continually testing them to find the best possible answer and then build upon that knowledge, seeing the interconnection between schools of thought and how they might influence one another. Scientists such as Jabir ibn Hayyan emphasized an empirical method, meaning they focused on evidence that was found through experimentation and observation to support a theory, as opposed to merely meditating on the topic and reaching a conclusion. In other words, the only true things are that which can be proven through demonstration. Interestingly, this was the first philosophy that demanded that evidence be consistently true.

It was insufficient to base a claim on secondhand accounts. This held discoveries to a higher standard than before and ensured that scientists would not simply base their theories on the assumption of their predecessors' correctness. Further, it made sure each scientist took the time to fully understand each step toward his new field of inquiry. Experimentation took on new life during this time.

The RENAISSANCE

Many of the advancements of the Greeks and Arabs would go undiscovered, unrecognized, and unused by the nations and cultures of Europe until the twelfth century, more often known as the Renaissance. Latin translations finally became available, and the concepts of observation and experimentation spread among Western civilization for the first time in centuries, with the luminaries of the time adding their own opinions and methods. Some, such as Robert Grosseteste, wrote that verification was paramount in any discovery, insisting that it be applied both to processes that could be demonstrated as well as those that were predicted. Roger Bacon, a Franciscan friar of the thirteenth century, would bring these ideas to Pope Clement IV in 1267, enhancing the scholastic accomplishments of the Catholic Church at that time. This would prove vitally important in maintaining the relative harmony between matters of faith and science, as the rediscovered Aristotelian method was found to be compatible with Christian dogma and mythos, making it a tool without controversy.

Translated texts soon resurrected old schools of thought as well as aroused new debates and perspectives. "The Outlines of Pyrrhonism" brought classical skepticism into vogue. Skepticism, as a philosophy, can be defined as the exceptional doubt (or even denial) of anything being certain. This was less a method for

A drawing of Roger Bacon, a thirteenth-century Franciscan friar who introduced scientific methods to the Pope.

ROGERIVS BACO,
Monachus in Anglia

finding scientific or philosophical truths than it was a backlash against the presumption of knowledge, a kind of high tide of self-awareness. It stood in stark opposition to the Aristotelian method and inspired generations of scientists and philosophers such as Francisco Sanches, Michel de Montaigne, and René Descartes to search for newer, better methods for finding efficient, trustworthy facts upon which to base future discoveries.

The problem they faced was that Aristotle's method was too vague, more about establishing a foundation than explaining the particulars of how to find reliable information. Worse, the subjective nature of observation meant that it couldn't be trusted. What if it was observed in the wrong way or the wrong conclusion was drawn? It became harder and harder to trust evidence and develop theories, let alone support them. Even today, the debate rages on. The observer effect states that merely witnessing any event changes its outcome. The classic saying that best embodies this paradox is, "If a tree falls in the forest, and no one is around to hear it, does it make any sound?"

Francis Bacon would develop a method that insisted on testing and proving not only the main principles but all those related to them, establishing a connection between all associated facts and theories. By creating a history of experiments, comparing alternative theories to find the right one, a stable body of knowledge could be formed to work from. The hardest part of this was compiling records of experiments, documenting what had been tried and what had been assumed, then thoroughly testing all elements to find the ones that worked and moreover worked with each other. Theories began to support one another through demonstration.

Around the same time, Galileo Galilei was utilizing similar principles, emphasizing experiments as a method of research. What's more, he would utilize mathematics to demonstrate his findings, which was, at the time, unprecedented. The

Galileo Galilei was an astronomer, innovator, and pioneer of early gravitational science.

Aristotelian method focused on finding the cause of things in an abstract sense, while mathematics demanded a specific and demonstrable form. Unfortunately, his reliance on experimental results was not a popular school of thought at the time, and he had to couch his findings and theories in the trappings of Aristotelian terminology and understanding. Among his many subjects of study were the beginnings of what would eventually become gravitational theory.

The empirical, experimental method found its firm footing with Sir Isaac Newton, who established what he called his four "Rules of Reasoning" in his work, the *Principia*. These four rules are:

1. "We are to admit no more causes of natural things than such as are both true and sufficient to explain their appearances." This means that one can only accept the explanation for a natural phenomenon as fact if it is fully explainable, demonstrable, and proven. Doing otherwise distracts from better theories, and worse, can cause otherwise meritorious experiments to be conducted all wrong.

2. "Therefore to the same natural effect we must, as far as possible, assign the same causes." This is the other side of the coin, demanding that any given natural effect be identified and understood thoroughly.

3. "The qualities of bodies, which admit neither intension nor remission of degrees, and which are found to belong to all bodies within the reach of our experiments, are to be esteemed the universal qualities of all bodies whatsoever." Effectively, this means that what has proven true for us, and is confirmed by others, should be held as a standard to which others can refer reliably.

Sir Isaac Newton was a polymath and the father of early physics and gravitational theory.

4. "In experimental philosophy we are to look upon propositions collected by general induction from phenomena as accurately or very nearly true, notwithstanding any contrary hypotheses that may be imagined, until such time as other phenomena occur, by which they may either be made more accurate, or liable to exceptions." This is, perhaps, one of the most important statements of Newton's rules. He is saying that we can trust what we have learned up to the point where new evidence and discoveries give us cause to question previous facts. In essence, it means that we should always remain open-minded, always willing to try a new approach, continuing to test what we might otherwise take for granted as fact with new theories and methods, to ensure that we are always operating from sound scientific footing.

Newton further emphasized a need for modesty and specificity. A "theory of everything," which might offer a universal answer to be applied to all sciences, was considered too tall a task for any one natural philosopher to approach. Rather, he favored a more pragmatic approach, pursuing particular lines of inquiry. The work of a lifetime, Newton proposed, would be a part of the much larger body of understanding to which all scientists would contribute in their own ways. "'Tis much better to do a little with certainty, and leave the rest for others that come after you, than to explain all things." By proposing this focused, specialized approach, scientists could thoroughly research singular subjects, resulting in much more reliable, credible results that all others would benefit from. This dedication to detail redefined and reinforced the different schools of science, offering the path for in-depth discoveries never before possible.

To call Newton's work influential would be a gross understatement. It became the foundation for all that would follow, the standard that would influence scientific research into the early nineteenth century. Almost all contemporary sciences to follow would see their fields influenced by the methodologies and ethics Newton established over the course of his career, of which he would advance the field of optics, develop calculus, build the first practical reflecting telescope, and more to the point of this work, form the laws of motion and universal gravitation. Those discoveries alone would shape the nature of scientific advancement and the way in which we view our world, our universe, and ourselves, and how each interact.

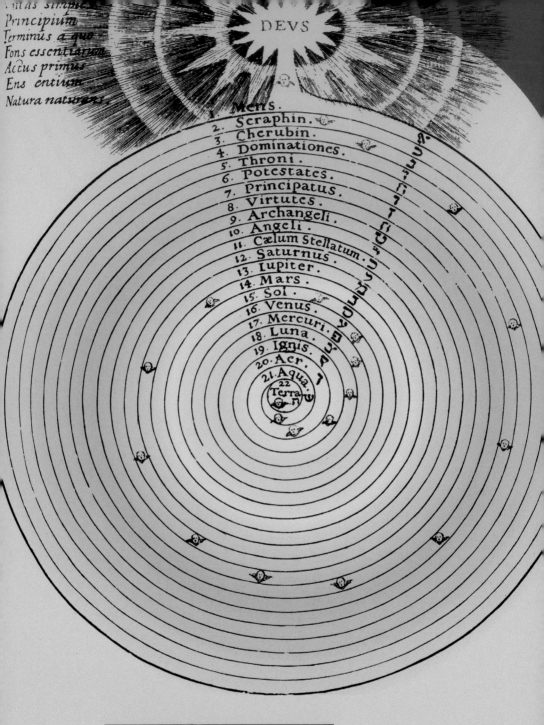

An early diagram of Aristotle's elemental interactions.

CHAPTER 2

The Science of Gravity

G ravitational science begins with the work of Aristotle in fourth-century BCE Greece. Aristotle composed a lecture known as *Physics*, where he worked to establish laws that would define the principles of change in all matter. This included the subject's size, its quantity, its coming and going into existence, and its motion.

Aristotle came to believe that the relative weight and motion of any object was determined by its composition of the four elements: earth, air, fire, and water. That means that things with a high ratio of air would rise, float, and fly, while things with a greater degree of earth would sink. Earth and water were the heavy elements, constantly falling, flowing, or resting reliably underfoot. If it was high and had no support, it fell. Air and fire were the light elements, as the air is obviously weightless in a purely experiential sense, and fire seems to rise up, with smoke pluming toward the sky.

It's important to note that Aristotle did not truly believe that all things were composed of those elements in a literal sense. These were not recipes for the creation of matter. The elements existed as a kind of set of abstract categories. You could compare this to food groups, for example. A strawberry is clearly not the same as an apple, but they are both types of fruit, while a loaf of bread and a cracker have more in common with each other than with the apple or the strawberry. It is one of the first examples of sorting different types of matter, comparing and contrasting their nature to try and establish patterns. Today it is known that matter is infinitely more complex, and we are capable of cataloging the composition of almost any matter down to its sub-molecular level, but this forms the first true exploration of the concept.

Aristotle observed the effect of gravity as well as anyone else. What went up came back down, after all. So he worked to find an explanation that fit his view of the universe. What he came up with was that everything had a natural place in existence. The four elements each had interactions with one another, and by observing those interactions, he defined their places in relation to each other. Earth was the heaviest element, and fell the farthest. If a hole was dug and a stone dropped into it, it would fall as far as it could until it rested at the bottom. Water formed the layer above it, since water always stopped when it hit earth and could be suspended in a bowl. Nothing else would stop it from falling or contain it. Air was lighter than water, as evidenced by bubbles rising upward. Fire, therefore, was the lightest element, which was demonstrated by the fire, itself, rising up in open air just as bubbles did in water. The only thing that was lighter than that was the moon or whatever mysterious force held it aloft.

By looking at his theory, a kind of physical model was established. Place, or the state where an element was in its natural state and unmoving, was defined by the locations that border it. The elemental composition of any matter could be found by seeing where it fit along this scale. Water contained earth, air contained water, fire contained air. Something that floats in water is more air than water, yet if it falls to the ground, it must be heavier than the air, as well. So, this natural motion suggested that anything made of air or fire rises, while anything made of earth or water falls. It was supposed that the highest point of all creation, known as the empyrean, was occupied entirely by fire and therefore explained the powerful nature of fire to create light, to burn, to warm, and to rise up toward the heavens, overwhelming and consuming the matter it came into contact with. Mythology stated that fire was a gift from the titan Prometheus, stolen from the gods on Mount Olympus and brought down to be given to humans for their use and prosperity. Seeing fires started by the strike of lightning from the heavens would have been more than enough evidence of this for them.

So what did Aristotle believe these objects were rising or falling toward, and why? His belief was that varied objects would settle and stop wherever they found their balance with the universe. Things moved because they were trying to return to a natural resting point. Those points were layered as explained earlier, but in a grander sense, Aristotle believed that earth and water were falling toward the center of the cosmos and that fire and air rose up and away from it. Many were willing to accept this based on theological principles but further because there was a certain mystical and indefinable quality about air and fire. After all, they defied quantification, filling lungs seemingly without mass or substance, burning or blowing, unseen or glowing. Comparatively, stones, dirt, and trees were understandable. A stone could be held, and it tried to go back to the ground where it belonged once you let go of it or removed any obstacles in its journey downward. Water flowed along the earth in rivers and seas, watering crops, keeping people clean, and sustaining their very survival. Fire burned and consumed but also affected matter, changing its nature so that metal could be worked, water boiled, and dough baked into bread, and offering simple warmth in the cold even as it turned wood into ash. One could not package fire, nor handle it directly. Of all the elements, fire must have seemed very much like magic.

One of the most important things to remember here is that Aristotle claimed all objects have their own inner gravitas. In other words, the source of any subject's gravity (and by extension all gravity) was in the object, itself, and not from an external force. This was an easy mistake to make, since the idea of global forces unifying all things was a bit of a leap to make for them. It's much simpler to assume that each object has a different kind of gravity all its own, which seemed to be proven by the difference in weight. A bag full of feathers was lighter than a much smaller piece of lead. Surely the lead was trying to return to earth, while the feathers could be swept by the wind to fly away. Surely that was how birds flew and weights worked. Without the concept of a unifying force, or density, or any of the ideas that would form gravitational theory, this was the only conclusion they could reach.

Of course, this theory suggests water would all be resting under the air. How could Aristotle explain rainfall? His answer was the same as those that explained the energy of all motion. Matter, according to his writing, held within it a potential for change that can be actualized by specific circumstance. Wood could burn if exposed to fire, and fire could be doused if exposed to water, for example, and in the case of motion, the movement of any matter toward its natural place. A stone resting on the ground held potential motion, which was actualized when it was away from the ground and no longer obstructed. The rain, in this case, was warm air that cooled higher up, becoming water and falling once again, changing its nature through exposure to its neighboring elements. The possible potentials reached far, from water becoming ice to earth becoming fire.

There was a fifth element, as well, which was referred to as ether. Ether allowed an explanation of both the movement of celestial bodies (any natural body outside of the earth's atmosphere, such as the sun or moon) during a time when the earth was thought to be flat, endless, and certainly the center

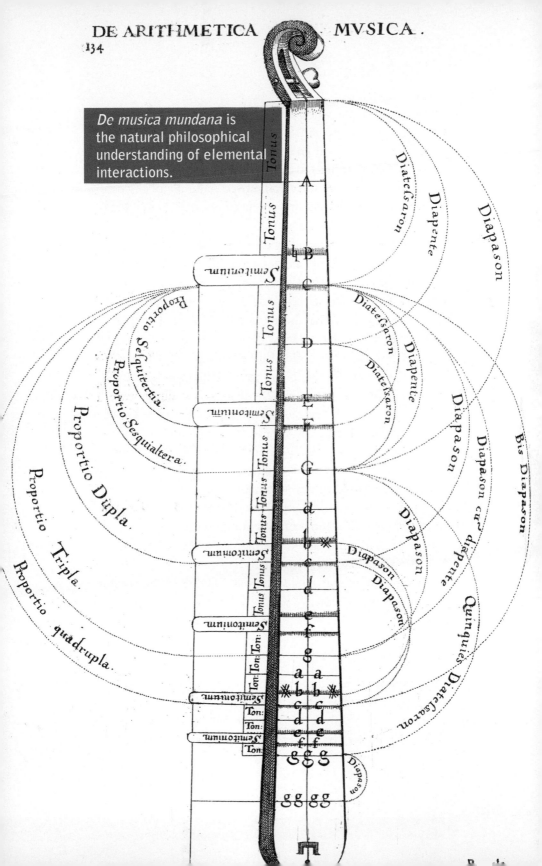

De musica mundana is the natural philosophical understanding of elemental interactions.

of the universe. The word "ether" is derived from ancient Greek, meaning "pure air." It was believed to be the air that was existing among the gods on Mount Olympus. This special element was not subject to causation or reaction, existing as a kind of independent force that moved naturally in circles, explaining the consistent movement of celestial bodies that Aristotle observed in the night sky.

Was this right? Absolutely not! But it was the first real attempt to look at matter as a sum of components, rather than as a singular, isolated object. People began to see that the observable universe was made up of smaller elements, and more excitingly, that those ingredients were shared between different objects. Most importantly for gravitational theory, however, is the notion that all things happen for a reason. Aristotle referred to it as cause. All of this is just one example of his idea of cause as the impetus for all motion in the universe, even if that cause was so abstract as "stuff goes back where it belongs." In the case of ether, there was no conceivable way to argue his point beyond offering up one that was equally unfounded and likely not as well-regarded as what might be put forth by so notable a natural philosopher as Aristotle. There wasn't any other theory to work from or to compete with, and it made enough sense to satisfy the question for natural philosophers for a very long time. Ether, in particular, would prove to be a fundamental flaw in scientific thought that would lead natural philosophers astray for a long time to come.

BRAHMAGUPTA

Later in India during the seventh century, mathematician and astronomer Brahmagupta was developing his own notions that, while incomplete, would help to eventually shape gravitational theory. While the first known writings of a spherical world come from Greek antiquity and provide only clues about how this was discovered, the idea persisted and reached Brahmagupta and other natural philosophers of the region and era. His own contribution to this was the notion that the round earth must somehow pull all other things toward itself as an inherent part of its nature. What is extraordinary about this is that it meant objects fall toward a central mass, and Brahmagupta supposed this meant that the earth, itself, generated the attractive force that must pull all things toward itself. The only thing that would stop things from sinking lower is the density of mass or other obstacles holding it up. While this might seem to support Aristotle's idea of a proper place for all things on a philosophical level, the scientific takeaway is that the earth generates an attractive force. Unfortunately, there is little else from Brahmagupta on the topic. Even his scant mentions of this revolutionary notion are only quoted by others who documented his works.

GALILEO GALILEI

Believe it or not, there would be almost no further thought on the topic for the next several hundred years, not until the sixteenth and seventeenth centuries, when Galileo Galilei, the Italian polymath and genius, would question Aristotle's assumption that matter falls at different rates depending on its weight. Until that point, it was considered a fact that a heavier object would accelerate and fall more quickly to the ground than an object that is lighter. The heavier the object, the faster it falls. For example, if one were to drop a heavy lead cannonball from the roof of a building at the same time that she dropped a smaller, lighter stone, the canonball, being heavier, would strike the ground first.

Galileo, according to legend, climbed the Leaning Tower of Pisa. Once he was at the top, he dropped iron balls of

An illustration of Galileo's legendary experiment on the Leaning Tower of Pisa.

A photo of the Apollo 15 hammer and feather drop experiment.

different weights, noting that despite the variation, they would strike the ground at the same time. While this story is largely believed by historians to be a dramatization, the conclusion has proven true. The actual, practical experiment may have been performed by Simon Stevin in 1586 and repeated many times since, perhaps most remarkably with a hammer and feather on the moon by astronaut David Scott during the Apollo 15 mission in 1971.

Now, the natural philosopher believes what he is able to observe and verify by that observation. There are plenty of things that might seem to argue against Galileo's results. For example, if one were to go back to the roof of that building and drop that heavy lead cannonball again, and compare the acceleration of its descent to that of a big chunk of Styrofoam, it's pretty likely the cannonball will hit the ground first. Fortunately, Galileo already understood the principle of resistance, which is the drag created when one kind of matter moves through or along another. The Styrofoam is lighter but has more surface area, slowing down because there is more resistance for it to cut through than the cannonball. In Galileo's time, a feather would have been the preferred medium to make an argument. After all, those feathers would be swept up in the wind instead of falling. The wind offers resistance. Except in a perfect vacuum, there is resistance in all places in nature, whether it is the wind, water, even the ground, depending on its density. Think about it: if a cannonball was shot and it landed hard on the ground, it would probably leave a crater. That crater is the result of the ground trying to resist the force of the shot. If the ground were not there, and that cannonball was shot into a bottomless pit with consistent resistance from the air, the ball would gradually accelerate at the same rate forever, or at least until the friction of resistance burned it away. This theory is known as the equivalence principle and continues to be tested even today.

Put simply, objects in motion do not slow down because it is their nature to do so but because another force is opposing it. That force can be particles in the air, the mass of water, the solidity of the ground, or anything else you can imagine outside of a vacuum. Lighter objects may fall slower because they are more prone to resistance than heavier objects.

The exciting thing about this theory is that it refuted Aristotle's idea of all objects seeking a point of belonging. A seed would not stop mid-air because it had reached the right elevation to be planted, for example. Drop it and it will fall until something stops it, whether it's the ground or your hand. The idea of a natural place for all things could not stand up to the proof of universal acceleration. Galileo's principle of inertia is "A body moving on a level surface will continue in the same direction at constant speed unless disturbed."

Alternative Theories

There were a number of other philosophers and mathematicians who had proposed their own theories regarding acceleration and resistance. Scientists and philosophers over centuries, including Lucretius (99–55 BCE), Simon Stevin (1548–1620), and Cristiano Banti (1824–1904), all proposed that unequal weights fall at the same rate. Banti even suggested that this could be tested with pendulums swinging at the same rate despite varying weights, or that different quantities of cork would all float in water the same way no matter how large or small.

The idea that objects fall at a uniform rate of acceleration as long as they do not meet significant resistance was not new to Galileo, either. In the fourteenth century, Nicole Oresme would develop mathematical laws for universal acceleration. Later in the sixteenth century, Domingo de Soto, a Dominican priest, suggested that the medium an object passed through would offer the same effect on all objects.

Inertia, too, did not spring fully formed from Galileo's mind before anyone else. In the fourth century BCE of ancient China, philosopher Mo Tzu had developed a vague concept of inertia. The first to propose a "theory of impetus" was Alexandrian philosopher John Philoponus in the sixth century, suggesting that it requires force to begin motion and that more force is required to maintain it or it will expire on its own. Jean Buridan brought the concept to Western natural philosophers in the fourteenth century, offering the bedrock of later theory on the topic.

None, however, had tested the theory or mathematically explained it until Galileo.

Now, this is all in relation to force and acceleration and resistance. You might ask why this matters in a study about the discovery of gravity. It's important to take into account the evolution of thought that made the very idea of a universal force possible, even plausible, to understand how the discovery was made. Without knowledge of force, resistance, and their interactions, it would be impossible to reach the conclusions upon which modern science depends today.

FALSE STARTS

There were, of course, any number of theoretical missteps along the way. In 1644, René Descartes insisted that there was no such thing as empty space. For him, a vacuum was not only impossible, but philosophically offensive. Descartes was a man of both the sciences and of morality and religion, and it was his emphatic belief that all things are connected. Any given truth must connect to another, and so on, so that any truth might eventually lead to all truths and ultimate wisdom and knowledge. In a more physical sense, there must be a physical connection between all matter, and the explanation must rest in an otherwise intangible force or matter that occupies seemingly empty space. Rather than thinking of it as a singular, amorphous mass as he might see water, he instead associated it with the structure of a great volume of sand, many tiny particles that were capable of shifting as a mass to move through and fill more solid spaces.

To this end, he believed that ether comprised the empty spaces in between tangible physical matter and therefore had to have structure, shape, and movement. Because this ether matter would be constantly compacted together, it would not be capable of moving about freely. Descartes suggested that it must be moving in circular motions, creating vortices in the ether. He felt that there was a difference in the matter

René Descartes was a natural philosopher and proponent of alternative gravity theories.

that point, Newton was among the vanguard of those who demanded that findings be a matter of supportable fact instead of assumption.

A number of other false starts can be found around the same time and even after the establishment of Newton's laws of gravity, some by Newton, himself. In his own words, "I do not feign hypotheses." This did not preclude his faith, however, as friends such as Nicolas Fatio de Duillier would later remark that Newton felt that gravitation must be the work of a divine influence. Bernhard Riemann believed gravitational ether to be an incompressible fluid in which normal matter represented a sink. If it was absorbed or destroyed, it could create streams that would cause local matter to be drawn to it. Imagine a pool filled with water. If one does a cannonball into it, the splash is a displacement of water, causing water around the displacement to rush in and fill the void. Unlike a splash, though, Riemann believed the missing ether would go to another dimension. Russian civil engineer and amateur physicist and astronomer Ivan Osipovich Yarkovsky had a similar belief but felt that the absorbed ether would be converted into new matter, so that the world is gradually becoming larger all the time. None of these theories are believed to hold any merit, however, because of the law of energy conservation. According to this law, energy can neither be created nor destroyed but instead can be converted into other kinds of energy. If that is the case, there is no way to explain how the energy in this theoretical model of gravity disappears, nor does it explain drag, as Newton pointed out. It also cannot be proven that the energy becomes matter, and it certainly has never been proven that any of the supposed ether moves to another dimension.

Pierre Varignon, mathematician and friend of Sir Isaac Newton, speculated that all matter is exposed to constant pressure by ether particles from all directions. Gravity would be a limit set by distance, suggesting that if matter was within that distance, it would be drawn back toward the earth, but if it could somehow be forced outside that distance, the pressure would be diminished. This was a surprisingly sound theory, as it accounts for the reduction of gravity as matter is drawn farther and farther away from the pull of larger masses, but once again depends on the as-yet unquantifiable nature and existence of ether in the first place.

This continuing reliance on an unsupported element in nature proved to be the eventual bane of most theories put forth during the 1800s and 1900s. Lord Kelvin and Carl Anton Bjerknes theorized that all matter has a pulsation in the ether, based on their observation that two objects that pulsate while suspended in a fluid will attract each other as long as they are in phase with one another. If the objects were out of phase, or pulsating at a different frequency, they would repel one another. Again, the theory was considered far-fetched because it demands that all bodies that are affected must be in phase with one another, which seems highly unlikely and is not at all demonstrable.

While there have been a number of advances in the field of gravitational theory, it is important to remember all of the theories and mistakes we have made along the way, if only to bear in mind this one, fundamental truth: our understanding is incomplete. No matter how sure a scientist may be of his or her research and conclusions, it must be remembered how many times through history others have been equally sure of their own conclusions—conclusions that are laughed at today as being foolish, incomplete, presumptive, or simply limited. One hundred years from now, it is entirely possible, and perhaps even likely, that students will read about modern beliefs and theories about gravity and wonder how the people of the twenty-first century could not grasp what they take for granted. A hundred years after that, the same will happen to them. But the continued efforts, to understand, to imagine, and to evolve, make up the building blocks of knowledge that will advance science and technological ability.

A portrait of Sir Isaac Newton, one of the most influential scientists of all time.

CHAPTER 3

The Major Players in the Discovery of Gravity

Isaac Newton was born in Lincolnshire, England, in the earliest days of 1643 (or, if using the old Julien calendar prevalent at the time, Christmas Day of 1642). Interestingly enough, Galileo Galilei died only months prior to Newton's birth.

Isaac was named for his father, a successful but entirely illiterate farmer who passed away three months before his son's birth. His mother was a young woman named Hannah Ayscough Newton. Hannah was the daughter of a gentleman, the sister of a man with a Cambridge University education. Although Isaac Newton Sr. was a successful farmer with land of his own and a small stone manor called Woolsthorpe, the fact remained that he was also a member of the working class who could neither read nor write. Marriage to him would have been considered, socially, a step down for Hannah. For better or worse, it was not a marriage that would last. Isaac Sr. died only six months after his wedding, leaving behind a pregnant wife who would give birth prematurely to a son not expected to live.

When Isaac Jr. was a toddler, barely three, Hannah chose to remarry. Her second husband was a man named Barnabas Smith, a well-off minister who was already sixty-three years old. Rather than choose to incorporate her son into her new family life, Hannah went to live with Barnabas alone. She left Isaac with his maternal grandmother, Margery Ayscough, with whom his relationship was frequently strained. This was the beginning of a nine-year-long period of abandonment and extreme neglect that, ultimately, was the source of a lifetime of emotional conflict and social anxiety for Newton. He considered this separation from his mother a traumatizing event, and he hated his distant stepfather. As a teenager of nineteen, Newton privately wrote down a "list of sins" he had committed up to that point in his life. Among other things, he included a moment in his early years where he had grown angry enough with his mother and stepfather that he threatened to "burne them and the house over them."

By the time Isaac was twelve years old, Barnabas the minister had died and Hannah chose to fully reunite with her firstborn. She moved back to Woolsthorpe, bringing along Isaac's three small half-siblings, whom she had given birth to during her time away from him.

Hannah arrived to find that Isaac's grandmother had been seeing to his education. He had been enrolled in King's School at Grantham, a town in Lincolnshire. To stay closer to the school, he was also lodging with a Lincolnshire apothecary who had been introducing the young boy to the laws of chemistry. It would appear that Margery had been preparing her grandson for a college education, but his mother had other plans. When Isaac was seventeen, Hannah chose to pull him out of school. Her intent was to turn him into a farmer who could work the land that Woolsthorpe was settled on, while she continued to raise his younger half-siblings. Isaac proved to not only hate this way of life but also be terrible at it. His mother agreed to allow his reentrance into school.

The PLAGUE and the APPLE TREE

Hannah's brother William, who had graduated from Trinity College at Cambridge University, sensed an inborn talent for intellectualism in Isaac. He shared these opinions with his

Trinity College Cambridge, where Sir Isaac Newton studied and later taught.

sister and, in 1661, successfully persuaded her to allow Isaac to enter the university as a student. Newton enrolled as a "sizar," in a program that was a seventeenth-century equivalent to the work-study programs of modern times. When he was not studying, he waited tables and cleaned the dormitory rooms of wealthy students. Given the amount of extra work that was a part of his daily life, which richer students did not need to take time away from their studies to worry about, it is perhaps unsurprising that the bachelor's degree awarded to him in 1665 was given without any honors or distinction.

Though the Scientific Revolution of the seventeenth century had already begun, very little of its core philosophy had impacted the education being received by Cambridge students. Contemporary scientific masters were discovering principles that were causing the Cambridge syllabus to become outdated. Newton turned to private study. Where his mathematics professor found Newton's understanding of Greek mathematician Euclid to be severely lacking, surviving notebooks prove that the young student was privately mastering the works of René Descartes, whose *Géométrie* was far more advanced than the mathematical concepts found in Euclid's *Elements*.

Shortly after Newton received his bachelor's degree, Cambridge was obliged to close down owing to health concerns caused by the Great Plague, the last major epidemic of bubonic plague in England, which killed one hundred thousand people, or about one-fourth of the population of London. Newton returned to Woolsthorpe and took the next two years to continue his studies privately. It was during this time, as his own master, that Newton was able to bring his mind to focus and lay the foundations for many of his later principles. "All this was in the two plague years of 1665 to 1666," he later recalled, "for in those days I was in my prime of age for invention, and minded mathematics and philosophy more than at any time since."

There is a widely believed story taught to schoolchildren that derives from this period in Newton's life. In the story, Newton is in his garden at Woolsthorpe sitting under an apple tree. An apple falls off the tree and hits his head, and he is suddenly inspired to realize the universal law of gravitation. This anecdote, though a nice children's tale, is probably not true. At the very least, it is exaggerated. It would be more likely to imagine something along these lines: Newton witnessed an apple fall from the tree in his garden. He realized that the apple had a velocity of zero when it was hanging from the tree, and

Sir Isaac Newton and the famous apple tree.

that this velocity became accelerated as it fell. He asserted that there must be an outside force causing the acceleration of the apple. The force is gravity, and the acceleration of the apple is caused by this gravity.

Whether or not this specific anecdote is true, the fact remains that this is probably the time in his life when Newton's first thoughts on gravity took root. It would take another two decades for those initial studies to blossom into his masterpiece, the *Principia*.

It is charming to note that, whether or not an apple struck Newton on his head, the apple tree itself is still alive. It is more than 350 years old and still growing apples each year in the garden of Woolsthorpe Manor. Enthusiasts have taken several cuttings from the tree over the centuries, and in this way, the original Woolsthorpe tree now has children scattered across England. One of them resides at Trinity College beneath the window of Newton's old room.

When Cambridge reopened in 1667, Newton returned and was elected a minor fellow at Trinity College. The fact that he was awarded the fellowship is surprising given his earlier lack of distinction, and one can only assume that the private advancements he made during his time away from school aided his efforts in achieving this new status. He achieved his master's degree the following year, and in 1669 at the age of twenty-six, he succeeded his former mathematics professor in the role of Lucasian Professor of Mathematics at Trinity.

PUBLICATION of the *PRINCIPIA*

Newton's most rigorous years of study were conducted in solitude, which was perhaps indicative of the fact that he had difficulty forming constructive relationships with his fellow scientists. He was bad at taking criticism, and throughout his life he had a tendency to consider any negative feedback in relation to his research as a personal attack.

It was one such incident between Newton and the English physicist Robert Hooke that may have acted as the catalyst for the publication of Newton's most important piece of work, the *Philosophiae Naturalis Principia Mathematica,* or *Principia* for short. Newton published the *Principia* after Hooke directly challenged his theories on planetary orbits. Newton had already considered Robert Hooke an enemy for some time. The physicist had previously criticized Newton's experiments on light and colors. Newton never forgave him for this and used this second attack from Hooke as impetus to complete and publish his masterpiece.

The *Principia* was Newton's most comprehensive, and important, publication. Published in 1687, it took only two years to write but was the result of more than two decades of research and thought. The main points contained in Newton's *Principia* were:

- Newton's theory of calculus
- The three laws of motion
- Newton's theory of universal gravitation

Whatever Newton's detractors had to say about his research before, the *Principia* was an enormous and revolutionary success. It secured him lifelong renown within the scientific community. A premature infant not expected to survive his first day in the world was now one of the founding fathers of the principles of gravity that continue to be in use today.

A SCIENTIFIC TYRANT

In 1703, Newton was elected president of the Royal Society upon Robert Hooke's death. Though he had been entrusted with a position of absolute power within England's scientific community, his inability to productively cooperate with other

PHILOSOPHIÆ

NATURALIS

PRINCIPIA

MATHEMATICA.

Autore *JS.* NEWTON, *Trin. Coll. Cantab. Soc.* Matheseos Professore *Lucasiano,* & Societatis Regalis Sodali.

IMPRIMATUR·

S. PEPYS, *Reg. Soc.* PRÆSES.

Julii 5. 1686.

LONDINI,

Jussu *Societatis Regiæ* ac Typis *Josephi Streater.* Prostat apud plures Bibliopolas. *Anno* MDCLXXXVII.

scientists tainted his later years. He had a wealth of political power and influence but frequently used it to further his own ends. Accounts from his contemporaries indicate that he aggressively manipulated the careers of younger scientists, advancing those he admired and harshly obscuring those he considered to be his enemies. As president of the society, he was able to denounce those who criticized him and even went so far as to publish the work of other scientists without their permission.

Undeniably a genius of his time, and lauded as such, Newton nevertheless went into an unhappy old age that was marred by a lack of close friendships, a lack of any personal relationship with a romantic partner, paranoia, and mental instability. He was afflicted with digestion problems in his eighties. At the age of eighty-four, Newton blacked out after experiencing a case of severe abdominal pain. He did not regain consciousness, and on March 31, 1727, he passed away in his sleep.

ALBERT EINSTEIN
Early Life

Albert Einstein was born in Ulm in Württemberg, Germany, on March 14, 1879—almost two hundred years after the publication of Newton's *Principia*. He was born into a secular Jewish family, with a father, Hermann Einstein, who was a salesman and an electrical engineer, and a mother, Pauline Einstein, who was a homemaker. He had one younger sibling, a sister named Maja.

Much to his parents' dismay, Albert's childhood development advanced at a slower than average pace in certain respects. He did not begin speaking until he was already three years old. When he did begin to talk, he exhibited speech challenges that he carried with him into elementary

Albert Einstein is considered the father of modern physics.

school. Though his parents may have seen these impediments as a bad sign, their son soon grew into an exceptionally creative child. He was incredibly curious and also developed a passion for music at an early age. He learned to play the violin as a child and carried the talent with him throughout his life.

Career as a Student

The Einstein family move to Munich not long after Albert's birth, and he began his elementary schooling there at the Luitpold Gymnasium. He did not mesh well with the academic institution's rigid educational style and felt isolated.

Einstein's first truly positive experience with education may have come in the form of an unofficial tutor. Max Talmud was a Polish medical student and friend of the family who was occasionally invited to the Einstein household for dinner. He began encouraging young Einstein's interest in science when he was still very young, presenting him with a children's textbook on the nature of light that inspired the boy.

The family left Germany for Italy, and then Switzerland. Einstein entered the Swiss Federal Polytechnic School in Zurich in 1896, with the aspiration of becoming a teacher of physics and mathematics. He received his diploma in 1901 but was unable to find a position as a teacher. He had a lackluster academic record and had irritated many of his professors with a habit of skipping class and studying independently. With no teaching prospects in sight, Einstein accepted a position as a technical assistant in the Swiss Patent Office. He continued his physics research independently while holding down a steady job.

Children and Marriage

It was during his time in Zurich that Einstein became close to a young woman named Mileva Maric, a Serbian physics student his parents strongly disapproved of due to prejudices against her ethnic background. Einstein did not take their disapproval very seriously, and he developed a strong bond with Maric. They exchanged long correspondence letters, and in them he shared many of his scientific ideas with her.

In 1902, Maric gave birth out of wedlock to Einstein's child, a daughter they named Lieserl. Today, the fate of Einstein's firstborn child is a mystery. It is believed that she may have been given up for adoption or else raised by relatives of Maric. Whatever the case, history is silent. Einstein married Maric one year later, and they went on to have two sons they raised together, Hans and Eduard.

The marriage was unhappy, and the couple would divorce in 1919. Einstein had been having an affair with a cousin named Elsa Löwenthal and would marry her that same year after his divorce had been finalized. He was equally unfaithful to his second wife and continued having affairs outside of marriage.

Year of Miracles

Historians and modern scientists regard 1905 as Einstein's Annus Mirabilis, his "year of miracles." This was the year that changed Einstein's life, the year that lifted him up from an unknown worker in a patent office and made him a figure in the public eye.

Within the span of one year, Einstein wrote a total of four physics papers. All of them showed remarkable genius, and all of them were accepted for publication in one of the leading scientific journals of the time, the Annalen der Physik. The subjects of the four papers were the photoelectric effect, Brownian motion, the special theory of relativity, and the relationship of matter to energy. It was the fourth paper that first debuted Einstein's famous equation of $E = mc^2$.

The "Miracle Year" was the beginning of a new life for Albert Einstein. It was the same year that he received a doctoral degree and the beginning of a long string of success for Einstein, who was still only in his late twenties.

In 1908, Einstein was made a Privatdozent (someone who can teach and supervise PhD students independently) at the University of Bern. In 1909, he was appointed Professor Extraordinary at Zurich. In 1911, he became professor of theoretical physics at Prague. In 1914, he was appointed not only to a professorship at the University of Berlin, but was also made the director of the Kaiser Wilhelm Physical Institute. For Einstein, all of this was just a warmup. It was not until the following year, 1915, that he completed what he personally considered to be his life's work.

Where Einstein and Newton Meet

In November of 1915, at the Prussian Academy of Sciences, Einstein presented his completed general theory of relativity. The general theory of relativity, which is a theory of gravitation, proposes that the observed gravitational effect between masses results from their warping of space-time.

Albert Einstein shares the equation for the theory of relativity.

For more than two hundred years prior to November of 1915, Newton's law of universal gravitation was the theory that science accepted as valid. Einstein understood that Newton's law was inherently shortsighted and that concepts like space and distance were not absolute (universally accurate regardless of relations to other things) but relative (considered in relation or in proportion to something else). He believed that his own theory would allow for greater accuracy when predicting planetary orbits, would provide answers to anomalies that Newton's law could not explain, and offered a more encompassing explanation of how gravitational forces functioned.

In May of 1919, British astronomer Sir Arthur Eddington utilized a solar eclipse to test Einstein's theory by observing stars that were close to Earth's sun. He found that Einstein's predictions were correct and that Newton's were inaccurate. A torch had been passed down from more than two centuries in the past, and the already successful Einstein was now rocketed to worldwide fame. Two years later, he became the winner of the Nobel Prize for Physics.

Targeted by Hitler

As Einstein was rising to fame, so too was Adolf Hitler and his Nazi Party. The Nazis exerted political pressure on the German scientific community, forcing many of its members to denounce Einstein's work, referring to it as "Jewish physics." As life in Germany became increasingly difficult for the Jewish community in the years leading up to World War II, Jewish citizens became banned from holding positions at universities, as well as many other official posts. Einstein became targeted by the Nazi Party for assassination. In 1933, he accepted a position at Princeton University in America. He was granted permanent residency in America in 1935 and would never return to his native country again.

Role in World War II

Einstein was one of many concerned about the possibility of a Nazi super weapon. Following the discovery of nuclear fission by scientists in Germany in 1939, Einstein and his student and fellow physicist Leo Szilard wrote to President Franklin D. Roosevelt, addressing their concerns and encouraging him to take steps for the United States to begin the production of its own nuclear weapons.

It is interesting to note that, despite these urges to Roosevelt, Einstein himself held pacifistic beliefs. Leo Szilard would go on to take part in the Manhattan Project, the famously grim American endeavor that would produce the first atomic bomb. Einstein himself declined to take any direct part in the production of an American super weapon. He did, however, make large financial donations to the American military by auctioning off some of his manuscripts.

Political and Social Activism

After learning of the devastation in Japan that the bombs produced by the Manhattan Project had caused, Einstein became appalled with the idea of atomic usage. He and Szilard founded the Emergency Committee of Atomic Scientists, which urged that atomic weapons be maintained only as a deterrent to conflict.

In his newly adopted American home, Einstein came to recognize parallels between the way German Jews were treated and the way African Americans were treated. He became a member of the National Association for the Advancement of Colored People. Throughout the 1940s and later in his life, Einstein would actively campaign for civil rights, correspond with activists such as W. E. B. Du Bois, and speak out against racism—which he called a "disease"—in speeches to university students.

Later Years and Death

Einstein continued to explore and fine-tune his general theory of relativity in his later years, focusing on concepts such as wormholes and the possibility of time travel. As the physics community at large began to focus more on the problem of quantum theory, Einstein quietly withdrew from the scientific world at large. He continued in his position at Princeton, preferring the camaraderie of close colleagues. He was offered the presidency of the State of Israel but quietly declined, though he did help to establish the Hebrew University of Jerusalem.

In 1955, while working on a speech, Einstein suffered an abdominal aortic aneurysm. He was taken to the hospital but refused surgery, preferring to accept the fact that his life was reaching its conclusion. "It is tasteless to prolong life artificially," he stated. "I have done my share. It is time to go. I will do it elegantly."

Einstein died the next morning, April 18, 1955. He was seventy-six years old. Though most of his remains were cremated and scattered, his brain was preserved and currently remains at the Princeton University Medical Center.

Einstein's "One Great Mistake"

In the years since the detonation of the world's first nuclear warheads and their use in warfare, there has been a great deal of examination of the scientists who had a hand in the weapons' development, particularly of their feelings about having created the most destructive device in history. Linus Pauling, another prominent scientist in the twentieth century, wrote this:

> On 16 November 1954 I talked with Albert Einstein at his home in Princeton, for a couple of hours, about various matters, scientific in part, but especially about the world as a whole. When I said goodbye, and left the house, I stopped on the sidewalk and wrote two sentences in my notebook, in order that I would not forget just what he had said to me. One statement that he made that I noted is the following: "Oxenstierna said to his son, 'You would be astonished to know with how little wisdom the world is governed.'" The other sentence about which I made a note is the following: "I made one great mistake in my life—when I signed the letter to President Roosevelt recommending that atom bombs be made; but there was some justification—the danger that the Germans would make them."

A portrait of one of the world's greatest geniuses, Albert Einstein.

CHAPTER 4

The Discovery Itself

T he discovery of the proper laws of gravity as they are understood today cannot be elegantly summed up in one neat moment. Our understanding of gravity, much like most science, is constantly evolving and changing. But the scientific standard for the majority of the last hundred years has been established on two events, spearheaded by two distinct and famous historical figures: Sir Isaac Newton and Albert Einstein.

It is simple enough to hold to the legend that Isaac Newton observed the falling of an apple (or even that it fell onto his head as he rested in the shade of an apple tree) and began to ask a question that no one else had really addressed in a thorough fashion: why do apples, and all objects for that matter, fall? Why do things fall downward and not upward? What force is pushing it down, or pulling it to earth? Until that moment, it was almost unaddressed by natural philosophers, accepted simply as a fact of existence or explained away as part of a greater system that incorporated all of the elements.

As a student, Newton studied not only astronomers and mathematicians such as Aristotle, Galileo, and Kepler, but also philosophers such as Descartes. When his current field

A painting of Sir Isaac Newton.

of mathematics was unable to define the forces he sought to understand, he created calculus (along with Gottfried Leibniz). His book, *Mathematical Principles of Natural Philosophy* (*Philosophiæ Naturalis Principia Mathematica in Latin*), was published in 1687 and contained laws that helped explain the forces of the universe, along with mathematical models that would prove their accuracy. Newton explained that there was no difference between the objects on Earth and those that flew through the night sky, and the same rules applied to each of them, even if the scale of magnitude between them was so great. Through these laws and principles, he added to Kepler's laws on planetary motion and helped validate that the sun was the center of the solar system.

SIR ISAAC NEWTON and MOTION

The foundation of all of Newton's theories is known as the three universal laws of motion. While they do not specifically define gravity, they explain the rules that apply to any force acting on an object, whether it is someone pushing a ball down the road or Earth orbiting around the sun. All of these laws can be seen in how objects and people interact in everyday life.

The first law of motion states simply that an object at rest will stay at rest, and conversely, that an object in motion will remain in motion. The only way that motion will change is if there is another external force that acts upon it. This can also be called the law of inertia. If a driver were to get into a car and not start the engine, the car would simply sit still. If the car is driven up a hill, the driver will need to press on the gas harder to make sure the car doesn't slow down and stop.

Newton's second law is called the law of motion. It expands upon the first law by stating that when a force is applied to an object, the object will accelerate in the direction

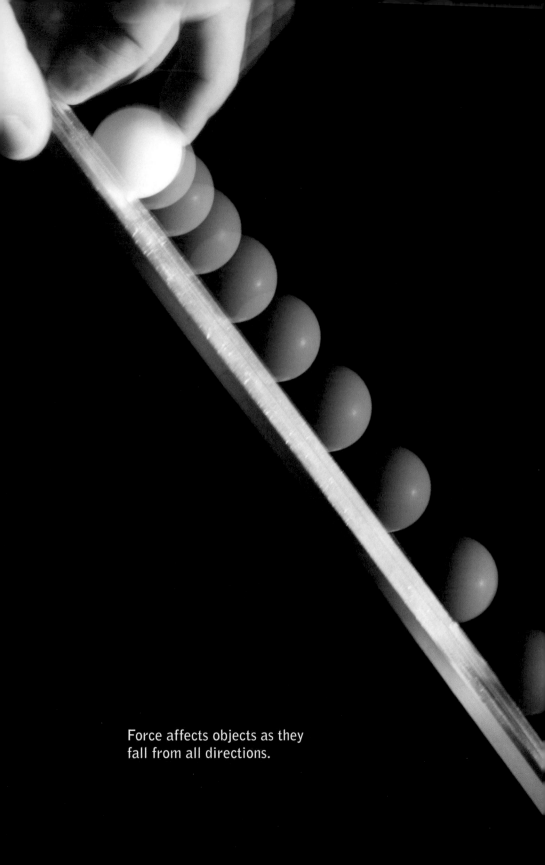

Force affects objects as they fall from all directions.

of the force. In fact, there is a direct proportion to acceleration and force. The harder you push an object, the more it will accelerate. He created a formula to define this relationship: $F = ma$. F, in this case, means the force applied, while m is the mass (or weight of the object) and a is the acceleration. When a car is sitting in a parking lot and someone presses on the gas pedal, the engine provides force to push the car forward by turning the wheels. The more the engine pushes the car, the faster it will go.

Newton's third universal law of motion describes how every force involves two objects. When force is applied to an object, that object also applies an equal force in the opposite direction. Or, more simply, for every action, there is an equal and opposite reaction. The tires on the car "push" the road in one direction, and the road "pushes" back, propelling the car forward.

With the three laws of motion and the fully developed math behind them, Newton was able to understand how every object in the world moved and interacted with each other. He was able to quantify that a specific force (gravity) caused objects to accelerate toward the center of the. But what about the planets in the sky? If Earth's gravity is pulling on the moon, why doesn't it simply crash into us? Galileo and Kepler had already conducted numerous observations and theories about the orbit of the planets and Earth around the sun. There had to be much more than the three laws of motion to understand the movement of celestial bodies. It was this line of thinking that led Newton to begin to develop his universal law of gravitation.

The problem that all astronomers have to deal with, of course, is that the sun and planets are too far away to be able to perform any sort of experiments to test theories of how they move through space. Newton had to rely on experiments and mathematical calculations that he could perform in his study. He knew that the moon seemed to always move parallel to the

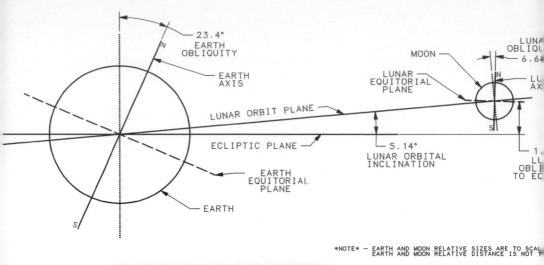

The following labels appear on the diagram:

23.4°
EARTH
OBLIQUITY

N

EARTH
AXIS

MOON

LUNAR
EQUITORIAL
PLANE

LUNA
OBLIQU
6.6

N

LU
AX

LUNAR ORBIT PLANE

ECLIPTIC PLANE

5.14°
LUNAR ORBITAL
INCLINATION

S

1
LU
OBLI
TO EC

EARTH
EQUITORIAL
PLANE

EARTH

S

NOTE — EARTH AND MOON RELATIVE SIZES ARE TO SCAL
EARTH AND MOON RELATIVE DISTANCE IS NOT T

The gravity of Earth pulls the moon in constant orbit.

surface of Earth and never changed distance. If gravity was constantly pulling on the moon, there must be another force that is working against it and holding it at the same distance.

For a practical example, take a stone tied to a string. If you spin the stone around your head, it is held in place by the string, but as soon as you let it go, the first law (the law of inertia) states that the stone should fly away from you, traveling in a straight line. Newton believed that if the string represented the pull of gravity from Earth, then it was the inertia of the moon itself that tried to keep the moon moving away from Earth in a straight line. From that conclusion, Newton believed there was no reason that same logic should not apply to all of the objects in the solar system.

HOLDING the PLANETS TOGETHER

Earlier astronomers like Copernicus, Galileo, and Kepler had already observed that the moon orbited Earth, while Earth and the other planets each orbited the sun. Newton's laws of motion pointed to the fact that if every celestial body had gravity, then the sun pulled on each of the planets just like Earth pulled on the moon. It was these laws and observations that led to his next major discovery: the universal law of gravitation.

From the second law of motion, Newton understood that, considering the size of the planets, it would take a massive amount of force to move them through space. The sun clearly exerted the strongest force, since each of the planets orbited around it, while the planets also exerted other forces on their own moons. The larger the object, the more force (or gravity) it seemed to create. What if every object exerted its own gravitational force? Smaller objects (like an apple) might create a force too small to observe or measure. In addition,

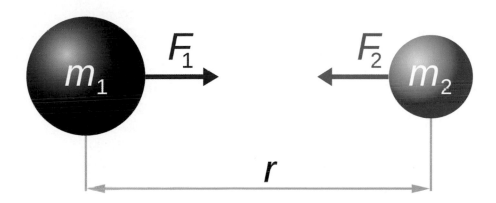

$$F_1 = F_2 = G\frac{m_1 \times m_2}{r^2}$$

A diagram showing the law of universal gravitation and the effects of force, mass, and resistance.

Newton could observe that even though the sun was much larger than Earth, the moon seemed to only move in relation to Earth's gravity. The moon was also much closer to Earth than it was to the sun. The distance between the objects clearly had a significant factor in how the force of gravity affected their movements.

Newton's law of universal gravitation states that the greater an object's mass, the greater its force. It also states that gravitational force decreases with distance. Thankfully, astronomers like Kepler had created formulas and calculations to determine the distance, speed, and size of the observable planets, such as Mars. Using that information, Newton created a formula to define the force of gravity. In order to do so, he defined a gravitational constant, also known as Newton's constant or "Big G." It was not until more than seventy years after Newton's death that the constant was actually measured by Henry Cavendish to be $6.754 \times 10^{-11} \text{ m}^3 \text{ kg}^{-1} \text{ s}^{-2}$.

The law of universal gravitation says that the larger the object, the greater the pull. If an astronomer were to go to the moon and jump in the air, it would take much longer for him or her to come back down to the surface because the moon is much smaller than Earth. Jupiter, the gas giant, creates an enormous gravitational pull around it, well over twice the pull of Earth. With this formula and enough information (such as the mass of Earth), physicists could also determine the force of gravity on Earth. Of course, this can also be measured through testing and observation by dropping an object and seeing how long it takes to fall to the ground.

The FORCE of GRAVITY

Over time and many experiments (including those conducted in vacuum chambers) scientists were able to determine that the force of acceleration of Earth's gravity is 9.8 meters/seconds2. That means, the longer that an object falls, the faster that it will accelerate until it reaches what is called terminal velocity. Terminal velocity is the fastest speed that something can fall from the force of gravity, and it is usually determined by the amount of air resistance that the object creates. That is why someone using a parachute falls much slower to the earth than a bowling ball. The parachute creates a large amount of air resistance, keeping the person from falling too fast. The force of gravity applied to both objects, however, is exactly the same.

UNDERSTANDING the "WHAT," BUT NOT the "WHY"

With these laws and formulas, published in his *Principia Mathematica*, Newton defined and quantified gravity as one of the forces of the universe. His work would be the basic foundation of all science and mathematics for more than the next two hundred years. Even today, Newton's laws and theories are used by mathematicians, astronomers, and physicists in their everyday work. But one of the most interesting things about Newton's work is that he himself had some doubts. While his formulas clearly defined the motions of objects, he did not understand how objects could affect each other over such a great distance through the vacuum of space. He could explain the force of gravity, but he could not identify the cause or source. In fact, he saw the problem as a philosophical one, as much as it was a math problem. Later on, other cases would be found (such as the orbit of the planet Mercury) that would seem to point to something else going on, but Newton's theories were still accurate for large objects. To unravel those mysteries, the world would have to wait for more than two centuries.

After Newton's discoveries, scientists and astronomers had an accurate, verifiable method for how gravity worked, not only on Earth, but also in space. His math could forecast the motion of objects through the night sky and was even used to predict the existence of the planet Neptune, long before it was able to be observed, simply because of the effect that gravity had on the orbit of nearby Uranus. However, alongside Newton's discoveries, other scientists were just beginning to experiment with theories about energy, particularly the concept of electromagnetism, or the understanding of things like light, electricity, and magnetic fields.

Another question that Newton couldn't answer was how gravity (or light) could move through a vacuum. Scientists still believed that a mysterious, yet undetected substance called "ether" existed that light was able to move through as it traveled through space. As telescopes and measuring equipment became more precise, small discrepancies also became apparent. The most widely recognized of these was the orbit of Mercury. At first, it was thought that there was simply another unobserved planet (much like Neptune), but time after time nothing was ever found. Then, in 1905, Albert Einstein would publish a series of articles that would change how scientists understood the very building blocks of the universe.

The THEORY of RELATIVITY

Albert Einstein was a German physicist who, during his lifetime, published a series of papers that would redefine gravity and how it affects matter. He is best known for his equation $E = mc^2$, which proves that matter and energy can never be created or destroyed, only changed from one state to another. At the time, many other physicists sought to understand and explain the apparent problems that were happening with some their experiments. There seemed to be gaps, or errors in how they predicted the movement of objects in the universe. Sometimes, these errors were explained away as problems with instruments used to measure the results,

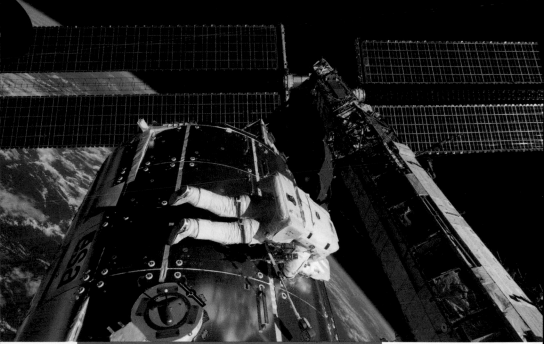

The understanding of gravitational sciences makes space exploration possible.

or that the calculations and formulas had errors that would account for the discrepancy. Einstein decided that it was not the experiments that were wrong, but the mathematics and theories behind them.

Like Newton, Einstein had to begin his work by establishing some fundamental laws about how the universe works. He wanted to come up with a system that could incorporate many of the currently proven theories around not only gravity, but also light and electromagnetism. Many experiments seemed to disprove certain theories, but rather than assume that the experiment was faulty, he postulated theories that proved them accurate. After many years of research and complex mathematical equations, he published his theory of relativity in 1916. In his work, he explained the idea of general and special relativity and defined the idea of space-time. This work helped to reshape our understanding of not only gravity, but of time and the universe as a whole.

The THEORY of SPECIAL RELATIVITY

The first part of the theory of relativity was called the theory of special relativity, and it is comprised of two main principles. The first is the principle of relativity, and it states that the laws of physics don't change between objects that are moving at a constant speed (also called a frame of reference). While this might seem to be a simple statement, it had a profound effect on how scientists perceived and measured the world around them. For example, even though you may feel that you are stationary, you know that Earth itself is not only rotating but also orbiting the sun, and the sun is moving along the Milky Way galaxy, spinning from its galactic core. However, from your perspective, and as far as the laws of physics around you are concerned, things are stationary. From a different frame of reference, such as an astronaut orbiting the planet, it is clear to him that you are moving along with the surface of Earth. So how did this change how scientists understood gravity? Einstein invalidated the existence of ether by saying that it didn't need to exist in order to explain how gravity and light operated.

Since the laws of physics are relative, the measurements depended only on the object and the observer. If two people were in a car moving down the highway without any windows, it might seem that they weren't moving at all. If one was to throw a ball to the other, the ball would be moving at a normal speed. However, someone outside the car would see the ball moving incredibly fast. In fact, she would probably measure the ball moving faster than the car, since it needed to accelerate to get from one person to another.

The second principle of special relativity says that the speed of light (in a vacuum) is constant in all frames of reference. If the laws of physics don't change, then the speed

Geosynchronous orbit requires constant adjustments.

of light doesn't change either. While at first glance this might sound the same as the first principle, up until that point, light and electromagnetism were viewed as separate from gravity. There was no singular theory that applied to both of them equally. But this isn't the case for light. Light always travels at the same speed. So what's actually happening?

As an object accelerates, especially as it gets closer to the speed of light, reality as it is understood (space and time) will begin to change between an observer and the object in motion. Because the laws of physics can't change for each object (they have their own frame of references), each object will have its own unique experience of space and time. Some of the strange situations that can happen for different observers because of special relativity include simultaneous events happening at different times and even time moving at different rates. Some of these strange events, such as twins aging at different rates, seem impossible, but Einstein and other scientists have been able to prove both mathematically and through observation that this theory is quite sound.

The Twins Paradox and GPS Satellites

The origin of the twins paradox arises from Einstein's predictions regarding special relativity. He predicted that if two clocks (A and B) showed exactly the same time and then one (clock B) moved away and then came back to the first clock, the moving clock (clock B) would have a different time. Time would have moved slower, due to the fact that the moving object had a different frame of reference. The faster and farther away clock B moved, the larger the time difference. Apply this situation to a set of human identical twins. The twin that accelerated away and then moved back would have aged slower than the twin who didn't move. Einstein didn't consider this a paradox at all. In fact, he considered it a completely natural consequence of how relativity worked. Other scientists used Einstein's computations to give specific examples of how much of an impact on the difference in the ages of the two twins was caused.

While this experiment might seem strange, there are actually numerous examples of how it has been proven and impacts our lives today. The GPS satellites that orbit Earth have very precise atomic clocks that are used to help compute location and distance with objects on the ground. However, since the satellites are in orbit, they have to travel a greater distance and at a much higher speed than an object on the surface. Over time, this difference causes the clocks on the satellites to become out of synchronization, and they need to be adjusted on a regular basis.

The THEORY of GENERAL RELATIVITY

The theories and mathematics used in Einstein's theory of special relativity eventually became a building block in his creation of a theory of general relativity. While special relativity explained some of the foundational theories about the universe and how scientists can measure and observe the forces of the universe (especially related to the speed of light), it didn't really explain the forces themselves.

Although an object on the surface of Earth might look stationary, it is sitting on the surface of a spinning Earth that is also orbiting the sun at an incredible speed. A scientist measuring the object might show that it has no acceleration or motion. To someone looking at the stars through a telescope, it cannot be easily determined if the stars are orbiting around the planet or if the planet itself is moving. In fact, if Earth were to suddenly change its orbit, it is quite possible astronomers might not notice any significant change, even though the distances changed might be massive. Someone on a roller coaster might think that she was in zero gravity as she quickly descend over a hill. Even astronauts on the International Space Station look like they are floating weightless in space, even though they are orbiting Earth at incredible speeds. All of these things have to do with the frame of reference or relativity of each object or person. Although Einstein didn't have roller coasters or space stations, he was able to observe and imagine scenarios like these.

FREE FALL and the FORCES of GRAVITY

To an astronaut orbiting Earth, there is no gravity. If the ship were to fire its rockets, the astronaut would feel that force pushing against him. Because of Newton, we know that inertia would push against the ship, trying to keep the astronaut in place. There would be no way for the astronaut to tell the difference between the force of the rockets and the force of gravity. To the observer, they are exactly the same. This understanding was named the equivalence principle and was the key to Einstein's theory of general relativity. It states that an observer cannot tell any difference between gravity and another force acting on it in a similar fashion (accelerating at the same speed of 1g), meaning that gravity is just like every other force in the universe. In some circumstances (such as when objects are in free fall), there isn't even any way to measure that gravity exists because all of the objects that are falling have the same frame of reference (just like people throwing a ball in a car).

If there is actually no unique force called gravity, then what is happening? Why do objects move toward each other? Why do larger objects seem to exert more force than smaller ones?

Most of Einstein's theories include detailed mathematical formulas. Ten of his formulas are part of the general theory of relativity and are called the Einstein field equations, or EFEs. They help describe how mass, energy, and gravity interact with each other. Using these equations, Einstein helped draw a map of how matter and energy interact with each other. One of the key concepts of this interaction is the idea of space-time.

SPACE-TIME

While it's easy to understand space and how to describe where something is located, we also exist in another dimension that we call time. Time tells us precisely when we are at a certain location. Scientists in the early 1900s began to understand that both space and time were part of an object, and they couldn't separate the two of them anymore than they could describe a three-dimensional object without describing how tall it is. This is especially important in physics because you need to understand what forces are being applied to an object and if it is moving or accelerating.

Space-time is a mathematical model that is used to describe all of the aspects of an object in the universe. By using space-time, models of the universe can be built that describe everything using the same terms and formulas. The concept of space-time is key to Einstein's theories because it is truly the foundation of the universe itself. It is not simply a way to describe an object, it is the paper that the universe is drawn on and that every object travels across.

GRAVITY and the CURVATURE OF SPACE-TIME

Einstein theorized that it wasn't so much that objects themselves were creating the force of gravity. Instead, he proposed all matter actually changing the properties of space-time. The larger the object, the more space-time curves toward it. Objects that seem to be falling and accelerating aren't changing their speed. They are actually staying in the same place, but space is bending and moving around them. The larger the object, the more space bends, "accelerating" objects toward it. Because we are inside of space, we can measure the value, but there is no actual "force" of gravity. Gravity is just our way of understanding how matter curves the space-time around us.

This effect of warping space-time also helps explain why objects aren't affected by the spin of Earth or the orbit of Earth around the sun. Earth is warping space-time around us and pulling us toward the center. We are held onto the surface of Earth by this "force," and that warping keeps us from feeling the effects of the other forces around us. The ground quite literally pushes up on us and keeps us in place.

PROVING the THEORY of RELATIVITY

Just like Newton's laws of motion, Einstein's theory didn't just explain gravity, it explained how the entire universe works. Many of Einstein's ideas couldn't be definitely proven or disproven because there was no technology to test the results. However, many scientists did use the theories and formulas to expand their own ideas of how the different forces of the universe interact with each other. Einstein was able to use his theories to explain some of those curious anomalies that other scientists had discovered. One example was the irregularities in the orbit of Mercury that had been known about since Newton.

One of the most famous experiments to prove Einstein's theories was conducted by Sir Arthur Stanley Eddington. In 1919 he led an expedition to an African island called Principe. There, he carefully measured and studied starlight during a total solar eclipse. Since the light of the sun was totally blocked by the moon, it allowed the stars closest to the sun (where they would normally be far too dim) to be seen. His findings proved that light itself was bent by the gravitation of the sun. It was Eddington's experiment that confirmed the Einstein field equations, and it was Eddington who led the charge to convince the scientific community of the validity of Einstein's theories.

However, it would be many years later in the 1950s and 1960s when scientists were able to use newer technology and sensory equipment such as telescopes to validate and expand upon Einstein's theories, the prediction of the existence of black holes being one of the most well known. Black holes are areas in space where the gravitational forces are so strong, not even light can escape.

Today, the theories of both Newton and Einstein are used in everyday work by scientists and physicists to explain the nature of gravity and the forces of the universe. However, there are still some notable gaps in their ability to model the behavior of very small objects. In the past one hundred years, a new field has arisen called quantum mechanics to help try and understand these interactions and to give us a new view into the forces of gravity.

Finding Gravitational Waves

More than one hundred years ago, Albert Einstein made predictions and theories about the nature of the universe, but humanity lacked the technology to be able to prove or disprove them. Just recently, physicists at the Laser Interferometer Gravitational-Wave Observatory (LIGO) were finally able to prove one of Einstein's most elusive theories: gravitational waves. Normally, these gravitational waves are too small and weak to be definitively measured, although their existence has been demonstrated in the 1970s and 1980s. Einstein proposed that if two black holes were ever to orbit and then collide, the release of gravitational energy would be much stronger than normal for the briefest of instants.

The LIGO observatory is a pair of L-shaped structures, one in Washington State and one in Louisiana, approximately 1,900 miles (3,058 kilometers) apart. Mirrors are carefully placed at the ends of each 2.5-mile-long (4 km) arm, mounted with numerous sensors and tools designed to eliminate the effect of vibrations. A laser is then bounced from one end of the arm to the other, with a detector combining and measuring them at the end. If there is no change, the lasers cancel each other out. However, if there is even the slightest change in the distance, the two lasers would interfere with each other, and this interference could be "heard" by the detector.

On September 14, 2015, both observatories recorded a disturbance. After months of studying data, the scientists confirmed that the gravitational waves had been caused by two black holes colliding. One of Einstein's greatest predictions had been proven.

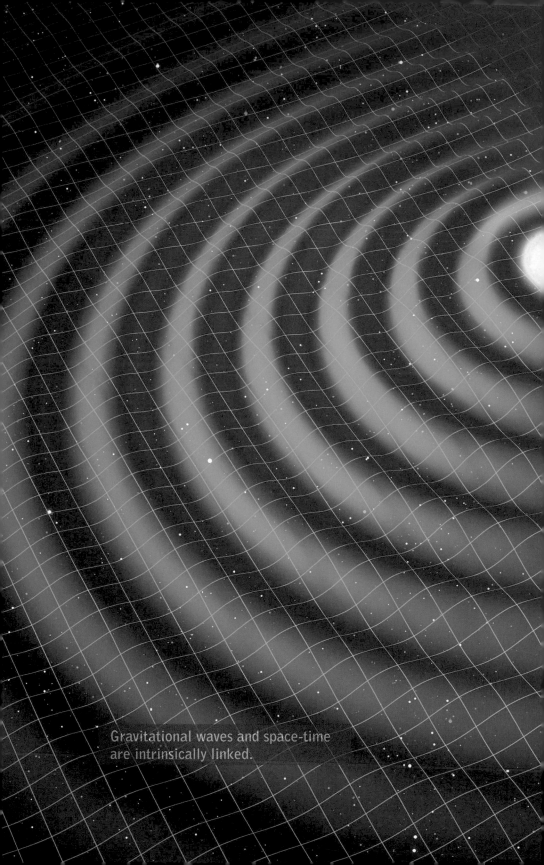
Gravitational waves and space-time
are intrinsically linked.

CHAPTER 5

Influence of Gravity Today

Is gravity just something that causes objects to attract? Perhaps, but gravity is also something that can be incredibly useful. Some species of bird have been observed dropping clams or nuts from large heights to crack shells, which is quite impressive. Still, it can easily be said that no other species on the earth has learned to exploit the effects of gravity like humans have. Even before we understood how it worked, we knew that we could make gravity work for us. Gaining a better understanding of gravity has only pushed our technologies and sciences even further.

Today we have a much better understanding of how gravity is everywhere and affects so very many things. Thus, learning more about how gravity works and utilizing its effects is still crucial to improving the future of our everyday lives. Everything from calculating the amount of fuel needed for trucks full of cargo to simple things like filling a balloon with helium so that it floats relies on our expanding knowledge of gravity. In this chapter, we'll explore the exciting ways gravity is shaping the future of science and technology.

CLEAN and RENEWABLE ENERGY FOR the FUTURE

Given how far our understanding of gravity has come, and how powerful its effect can be, a person might wonder if humanity will soon be able to use gravity to freely generate energy in a way that is reminiscent of a science-fiction story. While it may sound a little far-fetched at first, it's certainly not a bad idea. Gravity doesn't produce any harmful chemicals or gases, and it's effectively everywhere. There's no inherent risk of the world ever running out of gravity. Using gravity to create energy without having to waste additional energy is a pretty difficult problem. The task would require some serious engineering skills and cutting-edge technology, right? Luckily for us, our ancient ancestors have already done the work.

Archaeologists have found evidence that water wheels were used in ancient Greece as early as the second century BCE. A water wheel is a large wheel made of wood or metal that has big blades or buckets along the outer rim of the wheel. The wheel is placed in running water, which then pushes the blades, thereby rotating a central axle connected to the wheel. Vertical water wheels utilize the weight of falling water as it passes over the blades to produce more energy than the horizontal type. This innovation was far more than just a technological advancement. Water wheels are the first man-made machines that used a natural force as their power source, and they changed the very concept of energy sources for our species, which had, until that point, consisted entirely of human or animal labor. It signaled a future where humans would harness the elements and automation would improve productivity. Water mills allowed civilizations to greatly increase their agricultural output and experiment with other sources of energy, like winds and tides. The technology was so useful, it would stay in use well until the mid-nineteenth century when the demands of the Industrial Revolution spurred the invention of the first modern turbines.

Staring in the late nineteenth century, following the invention and deployment of electricity, turbines would become a critical component in hydroelectric dams. By placing turbines connected to generators inside of massive dams and allowing the water to flow over them, a hydroelectric dam can generate large amounts of power. As technology has improved and dams have gotten bigger, they can now produce anywhere from a few thousand watts (kW) to billions of watts (GW). When operating at full capacity, the mighty Hoover Dam on the Colorado River is capable of generating up to 2 GW of electricity and powering more than seven hundred thousand homes.

Hydroelectricity currently provides 7 percent of the energy consumed globally and roughly the same percentage of the power consumed in the United States. The United States is currently outranked in hydroelectric power production by China, Canada, and Brazil, but many other nations are eager to begin their own hydroelectric projects. According to a report from the US Energy Information Administration, the nations of Vietnam, Indonesia, Bhutan, and Laos have commissioned a large number of ambitious projects aimed at harnessing the rivers in their lands. Furthermore, policies enacted by the European Union in 2007 are aimed at using more renewable energy and construction has been approved for hydroelectric dams in Norway, Slovenia, and the United Kingdom. Many other European nations are currently upgrading their existing hydroelectric facilities to meet demand.

Clearly, humans have been exploiting the falling effect caused by gravity for far longer than what might be expected. Some of our earliest and most lasting power sources, like dams and windmills, owe much of their utility to the effects of gravity. The inherent principles used in these technologies have essentially remained the same for more than two thousand years. Only our ability to implement them has been refined.

AIR TRAVEL

What goes up, must come down. It's a fundamental fact of the earth. Yet, there are some creatures that don't seem as affected by that as others. Birds, insects, and even some mammals have mastered the ability to fly thanks to their respective evolution. Yet for most of our existence, humans could only dream of taking to the skies. Without being able to go up and see for ourselves, we could never truly know what lay beyond the clouds.

Looking at many legends like that of the carpet of Solomon, Icarus with his wings made of wax, and the four griffins that flew Alexander the Great around his kingdom, it's clear how alluring the idea of flying was to our ancestors. Defying gravity wasn't just an attractive idea because of its practical uses. It had the potential for great social and political significance, as well. Thus humans have tried, with moderate success, to fly for more than two thousand years.

It wasn't until Isaac Newton published his laws of motion and universal gravitation that engineers had the last concepts needed for true flight. Though humanity had failed at most of its early attempts to fly, Newton's work allowed for a series of innovations in a relatively short amount of time. The first major breakthrough came in 1783 when the Montgolfier brothers mesmerized a crowd in Annonay, France, by lifting a duck, a rooster, and a sheep into the sky with a hot air balloon. Within the same year, the Montgolfier brothers would be sending humans on piloted flights over larger distances. Ballooning eventually became something of a fad in eighteenth-century Europe, but the technology never reached widespread use.

Just 130 years later, the Wright brothers would successfully launch and pilot the first heavier-than-air craft, the Wright Flyer. The Wright brothers' plane could carry only one person, but it was a motor-driven, fully functional airplane. By the 1940s, bigger, faster, and more technologically advanced planes were rushed into production by several nations for World War II. After the war, warplanes were repurposed for commercial flight, which quickly become a common commodity, making rapid international travel a reality. The ability to fly passengers and cargo around the world had an enormous impact on postwar economics and changed the way people viewed the world around them. Before commercial flight, visiting a nation on the other side of the world could take months. Commercial flights made it possible in less than a day or two. The world, it seemed, was getting smaller. Perhaps that is why experimentation in aeronautics became geared toward going higher and farther than ever before.

The 1950 and 1960s would see the last true pioneering discoveries in aeronautics for some time. Feats such as breaking the sound barrier and high-altitude flight pushed the very limits of flight in ways many thought to be impossible. The lessons learned during this era would be instrumental in the development of the high-speed, high-altitude fighter planes used in modern militaries, but they wouldn't have as much impact on the commercial airlines. Still, these innovations contributed directly to the rapidly expanding field of astronautics, or the science of space travel. It covers several unique sub-disciplines of science and engineering, all of which are heavily influenced by gravity.

SPACE TRAVEL

Mastering air travel was a necessary step in traveling beyond Earth, but one of the most important aspects of astronautics, rocketry, has actually been experimented with for more than a thousand years. Simply put, rocket engines are a type of propulsion system that function by expelling fuel in one direction to propel an object in the opposite direction. Thus, a rocket is an object propelled by a rocket engine. Rockets are a critical component of space travel but they have only been proposed of as a method of transportation in the last century. Originally, rockets used solid fuels (usually gunpowder) and were primarily used for entertainment or war during the majority of human history. The nations of history knew that the same astonishment brought on by a fireworks display could be just as effective for intimidating their enemies. While several innovations in the design of rockets, such as multistage rockets, would be developed throughout the centuries, it wasn't until 1898 that the idea of developing rockets to be a reliable method of transportation was seriously proposed by a Russian schoolteacher named Konstantin Tsiolkovsky, a man now referred to as the father of modern astronautics.

Rocketry was greatly advanced during the early twentieth century as the technology was again pushed to the forefront of weapons research, this time to create long-range weapons that could hit targets all over the globe. The development of these multistage intercontinental missiles ultimately started a competition between the two major world powers of the time, the United States and the Soviet Union, to see which nation could reach the greatest of heights. Today, the alternating and constantly escalating achievements in astronautics that occurred between these two nations during the mid-twentieth century is called the space race.

Gravity is also a very large part of astrodynamics, the study of orbital motion. This field is critical in planning space flight and relies heavily on understanding the effects of gravity. Spacecraft control must be able to keep a vehicle or satellite in its desired orbit and maintain correct orientation. Without the proper controls, a satellite could float off into space or burn up while reentering the upper atmosphere.

Having enough fuel for a mission is vital to every spacecraft launch. Conventional wisdom says that if you need more fuel you should just bring more fuel. While that might work for airplanes that can, in an emergency, glide short distances to save fuel, the same cannot be said for spacecraft that must launch straight up in space. The heavier something is, the harder it is to push into space, so spacecraft propulsion engineers work hard to make their designs as fuel-efficient as possible. Launch pads for spacecraft are even built closer to the equator because that part of

Earth is moving faster than the other parts (up to 500km/h faster than at the poles) and gives the vessel an extra push.

Of course once an object is up in orbit, like in a space station, there is no gravity, right? Well, not exactly. Things may float around in orbit, but there is definitely gravity in space. Objects wouldn't orbit Earth at all without gravity. So why do things float inside a space station? The reason is actually quite simple. Everything in the space station, including the station itself, is actually falling. Objects in orbit around Earth are in a free-fall and, since it is known that gravity causes everything to fall at the same rate in a vacuum, any object that isn't strapped down seems to float in mid-air. This state of free-fall is referred to as microgravity. Astronauts train for this experience in a specially designed airplane known as a reduced gravity aircraft. This plane doesn't actually lower the amount of gravity, though. Instead, it flies up to great heights and makes a controlled fall for twenty to twenty-five seconds at a time. The airplane will repeat this parabolic flight pattern, meaning that it repeatedly rises and falls, to simulate the microgravity astronauts will experience during a mission. Due to the extreme shifts in gravity and resulting nausea that astronauts experience while training in the reduced gravity aircraft, the plane is often, jokingly, referred to as the vomit comet.

Astronauts training for micro-gravity on a parabolic flight.

LEVITATION

Planes and rockets aren't the only way humans have learned to defy gravity. Levitation can also be thought of as a form of sustained flight. Magicians have been crafting illusions that appear to levitate or float objects in the air without mechanical support for centuries, but it's only been within the last century or so that several methods for real levitation have come into existence. The most common form of levitation is aerodynamic levitation, which uses gas pressure, sometimes just air, to lift objects. This type of levitation is used for entertainment such as air hockey, indoor skydiving, balloons, or transportation like helicopters, blimps, and hovercraft. Recently, aerodynamic levitation has become an important tool for scientific research. Lab scientists are able to use this form of levitation to move or hold incredibly small samples that may be sensitive to physical contact without needing to touch them at all.

Another form of levitation is acoustic levitation, which uses sound waves to lift small, low-density objects. Acoustic levitation is only used for small objects and will probably never be able to lift large or heavy objects in a way that is useful. This is because the amount of sound intensity (SI) needed to lift heavy objects is incredibly large. The intensity of a sound can also be thought of as a measure of how audibly loud a sound will be. High intensity sound not only damages human hearing but could damage internal organs or cause extreme physical pain. So why use it? Because even though acoustic levitation is currently the most difficult form of levitation to utilize, it's one of the least likely to affect the outcome of an experiment due to an interaction with gases or magnetic radiation. This makes it ideal for working on small, sensitive materials like microchips.

Another exciting form of levitation currently on the rise is magnetic levitation. This type of levitation uses either the attractive or repelling forces of magnetism to counteract the effects of gravitational acceleration. Electromagnetic suspension (EMS) uses powerful magnets that hang off of an object and curve around the bottom of a surface or track. These magnets are designed to be powerful enough to lift the object but not enough for the magnets and the surface to actually touch, thus allowing the object to hover. In contrast, Electrodynamic suspension (EDS) places magnets on the bottom of an object and along the full length of a surface. These magnets are designed to repel each other rather than attract so that the object can be lifted. The types of magnets used for these systems, electromagnets, are special in that they require an electrical current to generate a magnetic field. Electromagnets are far more powerful than most permanent magnets and allow more control over how strong a magnetic field will be. Magnetically levitated trains, or maglev trains, are the technology most commonly associated with magnetic levitation. These trains use electromagnets to float just above a guide rail and even use magnetism to propel themselves back and forth. Because a maglev train is not in contact with the rail while it travels, the train does not experience any friction other than wind resistance. This allows maglev trains to travel at much higher speeds than traditional trains and ignore most weather conditions that would impair older types of trains. Floating above the rails also means that maglev trains take less wear and tear from friction so they are also less expensive to maintain over time.

GRAVITY ASSISTS

There aren't a lot of places out in space for a space probe to stop and refuel. On top of that, putting too much fuel on a spacecraft makes it harder to launch into space. This makes every bit of fuel on a space mission critically important, especially since a probe might need to expend fuel in order to avoid danger. To compensate for this NASA began using the gravitational pull of large celestial bodies, like our moon and neighboring planets, to accelerate spacecraft. This maneuver is called a gravitational assist, or gravitational slingshot. Essentially, a probe flies toward a planet that is moving in the opposite direction of the probe. As it approaches the planet,

A commercially operated high-speed magnetic levitation train.

the gravity of the planet pulls downward and the probe gains speed as it falls. The probe's trajectory is eventually bent all the way around the planet until the probe is moving away from the other side of the planet, but in the opposite direction of approach. The probe is now moving in the same direction as the planet it fell toward, but it has gained speed from falling and is pulled around the planet into the opposite direction.

NASA began using gravity assists with the 1973 Mariner 10 mission wherein the Mariner 10 probe used the gravity of Venus to change the its trajectory and achieve an orbit that would repeatedly fly by Mercury. Since then almost every space probe mission has made use of gravity assists to save fuel, time, and expense when planning, designing, and carrying out space missions.

LEARNING FROM GRAVITY

Gravity may not seem like an obvious source of information at first, but gravity measure, gravity mapping, gravitational lensing, and gravity wave analysis are among the fastest-growing and most sought after information fields currently in development. The uses for these technologies range from detecting underground resources or structures to detecting new planets to weighing entire galaxies and even observing the history of our universe.

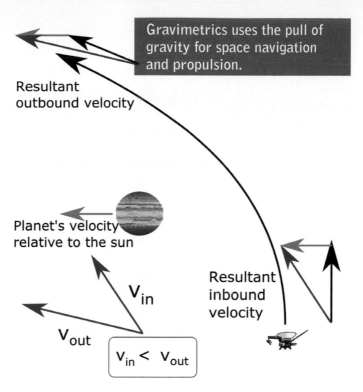

Gravimetrics uses the pull of gravity for space navigation and propulsion.

Resultant outbound velocity

Planet's velocity relative to the sun

V_{in}

Resultant inbound velocity

V_{out}

$V_{in} < V_{out}$

MEASURING GRAVITY on EARTH

Measuring the amount of gravity in a specific location on Earth can tell a lot about that place. It can reveal hidden bodies of water, buried structures, or vast mineral deposits. Gravimetry and gradiometry are separate technologies with the same overall goal of measuring the variations in gravity within an area in order to determine its material composition. Gravimetry does this by measuring the differences in weight that gravity causes using a device called a gravimeter. A gravimeter detects variations in the weight of small objects set atop a specially made spring. The device then measures the length of the spring to determine how strong the gravity in an area is. In many aspects, a scale can be thought of as a type of gravimeter.

Gradiometry measures changes to the acceleration caused by gravity rather than changes to the weight of an object. Gradiometers excel at measuring gravity while traveling at great speeds or over water, which has made them ideal for mounting on ships and aircraft. The range of gradiometers is much higher than gravimeters. As this technology improves, gradiometers will be able to detect subsurface materials at much higher speeds and greater heights with improved accuracy. This means we will be able to scan more of the earth without needing to drill down into the planet or needlessly waste time and resources on searches that might not yield anything useful.

Mapping the variations in gravity across an entire planet or moon can also be useful. Gravity mapping can track ocean flows, planetary ice mass, or liquid water on a planet. This is why, in 2002, NASA launched the Gravity Recovery and Climate Experiment mission. GRACE is actually two satellites that follow each other in orbit around Earth. Rather than measuring variations in gravitational acceleration or apparent weight, GRACE uses microwave ranging systems and precise GPS devices to measure the changes in distance between its twin satellites as they pass over a region. The stronger gravity is over a region, the more it will slow down the leading satellite, which will allow the trailing satellite to catch up to it. Then, when the leading satellite moves past the high gravity area, it will speed up and the trailing satellite will slow down. By measuring these changes in distance, GRACE has been able to provide gravity mapping of Earth for more than a decade. This information has proven useful to several fields such as climatology, early flood warning, water conservation, agriculture, ecology, glaciology, and many more. A successor to the original GRACE mission, GRACE-Follow Up, or GRACE-FO, is scheduled to launch in 2017 with hopes of improving its already impressive detection system.

USING GRAVITY to MAP the UNIVERSE

Much of the same principles applied to mapping Earth can also be applied to planets and moons beyond our own. The GRAIL mission, launched the same year as GRACE, used an identical set of satellites to map the gravity of Earth's moon. Perhaps more exciting, during the currently ongoing Cassini mission, scientists were able to deduce that Titan, the largest moon orbiting Saturn, has a liquid layer that could contain the components needed for life to evolve. This was discovered by observing changes in Titan's shape caused by Saturn's gravity. Since this technology is relatively new, gravity mapping may be able to reveal many more amazing parts of our planet and solar system as it becomes more common.

Gravity can attract everything in the universe, including light. Scientists have recently learned how to take advantage of this to see distant galaxies far beyond the range of our best telescopes. This phenomena, known as gravitational lensing, occurs when light is bent as it passes by an object with a large amount of gravity on its way toward Earth. Much like a telescope uses mirrors to bend and focus light, gravitational lensing focuses light from distant galaxies and magnifies distant objects far beyond the focusing point. Scientists have been able to use gravitational lensing to observe distant galaxies created during some of the earliest eras of the universe. It is likely that gravitational lensing will be essential for studying the full history of the universe.

Gravitational lensing may also help scientists find and identify planets orbiting distant stars in the future. By analyzing the way light is scattered during gravitational lensing, scientists can deduce the existence of planets near the point where light is being focused. This information, when further analyzed, can also reveal important information about said planets, like their size and composition.

General relativity predicts that objects with massive amounts of gravity that are moving through the curvature of space-time should create a sort of ripple in space-time. Einstein theorized that these gravity waves should be detectable but was unsure of how to detect them directly. These gravity waves would essentially work like the rings in a tree, giving scientists the ability to learn a great deal about a galaxy or solar system.

Gravity waves had never been directly observed until very recently. In February of 2016, a combined American and European experiment was able to observe and measure gravity waves for the first time. Analysis of the information revealed that the waves had been created by the merging of two black holes, which had occurred billions of light-years away from Earth. Just as Einstein had predicted, these incredibly dense, high-gravity objects had created a ripple in the very fabric of space and time. This groundbreaking discovery could very well lead to an entirely new field of astronomy based around gravity wave analysis. Objects in the universe that are completely invisible or do not emit any sort of light could soon be detectable by scientists. We may even discover new exotic types of matter that we haven't predicted yet. Gravitational wave astronomy is such an exciting field because of its incredible potential for reshaping our understanding of the universe.

The FINAL FRONTIER

It's been an incredibly long journey in reaching the level of understanding we have about gravity today, but that has never stopped humans from figuring out ways to make gravity work for them. The discoveries of brilliant minds like Newton and Einstein rapidly propelled science and technology further in understanding the universe and working with or against gravity. Everything from the power sources of ancient civilizations to airplanes, magnetically levitated trains, and the light-bending effect of gravity scientists are now using as a telescope to view distant galaxies relies on understanding the effects of gravity. If humans ever make the incredible journey to another planet or a distant moon, possibly even in a different solar system, the entire trip will be planned based on information gathered from the effects of gravity. It's clear, given all this, that the past, present, and future of our species is intricately linked to the mastering of gravity. Considering the astounding achievements of the last two centuries, it's very possible we'll see many more developments in the coming years.

Criticisms of General Relativity

General relativity is considered by most scientists to be a revolutionary theory. While there are disagreements about the implications of Einstein's theory, it's generally accepted that most of the major concepts it contains, like space-time and special relativity, are correct. Einstein credited legendary physicist Hendrik Lorentz with providing much of the groundwork needed for general relativity. Lorentz was an active supporter of Einstein's work, but Lorentz also believed that Einstein's theory was missing a key component. Lorentz believed in a constant frame of reference that wasn't affected by the effects of special relativity. This ether would be indistinguishable from the effects of special relativity and would have no real effect on observations. This would mean that ether would have the true time of the universe, not time that has been affected by special relativity.

The Lorentz ether theory was popular for a short time due to the complex and insightful work of Hendrik Lorentz, but it quickly fell out of favor after general relativity was published. Lorentz maintained his belief in the existence of ether, though he also continued to support Einstein's work up until his death. Much of the work Lorentz did is still highly respected today, and the difficulty in disproving the existence of ether means that there are still a few in the scientific community who also believe in the Lorentz ether theory. His work has also been used in a number of experiments meant to verify the effects of special relativity.

Chronology

Fourth Century BCE   Aristotle develops cause/effect theorem

Seventh Century CE   Brahmagupta theorizes a spherical Earth that generates an attractive force

Seventeenth Century   Galileo discovers that all objects accelerate at the same rate when falling

1609   Kepler's laws of planetary motion are born when Johannes Kepler describes how planets move around the sun

1643   Isaac Newton is born

1644   René Descartes insists on ether theory

1661   Isaac Newton enrolls at Trinity College Cambridge

1665   Newton is inspired to develop the universal law of gravitation

1687   Newton's Principia is published

1727   Newton passes away

1879   Albert Einstein is born

1905   Einstein publishes his famous $E = mc^2$ equation

1915   Einstein presents the general theory of relativity

1917   Einsten publishes a paper, theorizing stimulated
        emission, or the process by which an incoming photon
        of a specific frequency interacts with an excited
        electron, causing it to drop to a lower energy level

1919   Sir Arthur Eddington proves Einstein's theory
        over Newton's

1921   Einstein wins Nobel Prize for Physics

1960   The laser is invented using stimulated emission

2015   Scientists detect gravitational waves, confirming a
        major prediction in Einstein's general theory
        of relativity

Glossary

acceleration An increase in the rate or speed of something.

aerodynamics The study of moving air and the interaction between air and solid bodies moving through it.

aeronautics The science of travel through air.

astrodynamics Celestial mechanics applied to space vehicles.

astronautics The science of space travel.

constant Occurring continuously over a period of time.

density The relationship between the mass of a substance and how much space it takes up.

electromagnetism The interaction of electrical currents or fields and magnetic fields.

energy The capacity of matter and radiation to perform work, such as motion.

equivalence The condition of being equal in value.

ether A substance formerly believed to exist in all space, filling the gaps between physical matter and carrying light and sound.

force Energy as an attribute of physical movement.

galactic core The rotational core of the Milky Way.

gradiometry The study of variations in acceleration due to gravity.

gravimetry The measurement of weight.

gravitational waves A propagating wave of gravitational energy produced by accelerating masses.

gravity The force that attracts a body toward the center of the earth or toward any other physical body having mass, including but not limited to planets, suns, galaxies, and light.

inertia The resistance of any physical object to any change in its state of motion, such as speed or direction.

levitation The process by which an object is held aloft without mechanical support.

mass The property of matter that measures its resistance to acceleration and the measure of the number of atoms that compose it.

metaphysics Philosophy that deals with abstract concepts, such as being, knowing, cause, identity, time, and space.

microgravity Very weak gravity such as in a spacecraft.

natural philosophy The precursor to natural science, studying the world through philosophy.

orbit The gravitationally curved path of an object about a point in space, such as a planet around a star.

photoelectric The process of metals emitting electrons when light shines upon them.

propulsion The action of driving or pushing forward.

quantum mechanics The mathematical description of the motion and interaction of subatomic particles.

relativity The dependence of physical phenomena on relative motion of the observer and the observed object.

resistance The impeding, slowing, or stopping effect exerted by one material on another.

sophism Originally, to become wise. Currently, a false argument used to deceive.

space-time The concepts of time and space regarded as fused in a four-dimensional continuum.

turbine A machine for producing power where a wheel is turned by water or air.

vacuum A space entirely devoid of matter.

Further Information

BOOKS

Bortz, Fred. *Laws of Motion and Isaac Newton*. New York: Rosen Classroom, 2014.

Carroll, Sean M. *Spacetime and Geometry: An Introduction to General Relativity*. Boston: Addison Wesley, 2003.

Collier, Peter. *A Most Incomprehensible Thing: Notes Towards a Very Gentle Introduction to the Mathematics of Relativity*. Incomprehensible Books, 2014.

Dickman, Nancy. *Galileo: Conqueror of the Stars* (Superheroes of Science). New York: Gareth Stevens Publishing, 2015.

Hartle, James B. *Gravity: An Introduction to Eistein's General Relativity*. Boston: Addison-Wesley, 2003.

Kennedy, Alexander. *Newton: A Life of Discovery*. CreateSpace Publishing, 2016.

Manning, Phillip. *Gravity* (Science Foundations). New York: Chelsea House Publishers, 2010

Peterson, Kristen. *Understanding the Forces of Nature: Gravity, Electricity, and Magnetism*. New York: Cavendish Square Publishing, 2015.

Royston, Angela. *Sir Isaac Newton: Overlord of the Gravity (Superheroes of Science)*. New York: Gareth Stevens Publishing, 2015.

Schutz, Bernard. *A First Course in General Relativity, 2nd Edition*. Cambridge, UK: Cambridge University Press, 2009.

WEBSITES

How Stuff Works

science.howstuffworks.com/environmental/earth/geophysics/question232.htm

This website explains how gravity works and applies to everyday experiences.

Universe Today

www.universetoday.com/75705/where-does-gravity-come-from/

This website provides a clear, concise explanation not only of gravity, but its mathematics and applications. It includes a number of educational videos with wonderful illustrations.

Bibliography

Bergstrom, L. "Non-Baryonic Dark Matter: Observational Evidence and Detection Methods." Reports on Progress in Physics, 63 (5): 793–841, 2000.

Burt, B. C. "The Life of a Sophist." A Brief History of Greek Philosophy (http://www.e-torredebabel.com/greekphilosophy/thesophists-burt.htm).

Carlo Rovelli, D.M. Rote, and Cai Yigang. "Loop Quantum Gravity." Physics World, November 2003 (http://cgpg.gravity.psu.edu/people/Ashtekar/articles/rovelli03.pdf).

Clegg, Brian. *Gravity: How the Weakest Force in the Universe Shaped Our Lives.* New York, NY: St. Martin's Press, 2012.

Colosi, D., et al. "Background Independence in a Nutshell." Classical and Quantum Gravity, 22 (14): 2971–2989, 2005.

Crouch, Tom. Wings: *A History of Aviation from Kites to the Space Age.* New York, New York: W.W. Norton & Co., 2004.

Greene, B. *The Elegant Universe: Superstrings, Hidden Dimensions, and the Quest for the Ultimate Theory.* New York, NY: W.W. Norton, 1999.

Greene, Kevin. "Technological Innovation and Economic Progress in the Ancient World: M.I. Finley Re-Considered." Economic History Review 53 (1), pp. 29–59, 2000.

Hull, J. R. "Attractive Levitation for High-Speed Ground Transport with Large Guideway Clearance and Alternating-Gradient Stabilization." IEEE Transactions on Magnetics, 25 (5): 3272, 1989.

Jones, Mark H., and Robert J. Lambourne. *An Introduction to Galaxies and Cosmology.* New York, NY: Cambridge University Press, 2004.

Komzsik, Louis. *Gravity's Mysteries.* Bloomington, IN: Trafford, 2012.

Levin, Janna. *Black Hole Blues and Other Songs from Outer Space.* New York, NY: Knopf, 2016.

NASA Jet Propulsion Laboratory. *Basics of Space Flight,* Sec. 1, Ch. 4 (http://solarsystem.nasa.gov/basics/index.php).

NASA Reduced Gravity Research Program. "About the C-9B Aircraft" (http://jsc-aircraft-ops.jsc.nasa.gov/Reduced_Gravity/index.html).

Nussbaumer, Harry, and Lydia Bieri. *Discovering the Expanding Universe*. New York, NY: Cambridge University Press, 2009.

Peebles, P.J.E., and Bharat Ratra. "The Cosmological Constant and Dark Energy." Reviews of Modern Physics, 75 (2): 559–606, 2003.

Price, D. L. "High-Temperature Levitated Materials." New York, NY: Cambridge University Press, 2010.

Renewables 2011 Global Status Report. "Hydropower." REN21, page 25, published 2011.

Rote, D. M., and Cai Yigang. "Review of Dynamic Stability of Repulsive-Force Maglev Suspension Systems." IEEE Transactions on Magnetics, 38 (2): 1383, 2002.

Sadayuki, Ueha. "Phenomena, Theory and Applications of Near-Field Acoustic Levitation." Revista de Acústica, Vol. XXXIII. Nos 3 y 4, 2005.

Van Every, Kermit. "Aeronautical Engineering." Encyclopedia Americana, 1988. Grolier Incorporated.

About the Author

Kevin Czarnecki lives in Chicago, Illinois, where he works as a consultant, voice actor, game designer, and author. When not hiding from the sun, he takes every opportunity he can to travel, hustle another lecturing gig, speak at another convention, or otherwise make a nuisance of himself. This work would not have been possible without the assistance of Kit Pleasant, Chad Brunner, and Dylan Stangel.